Praise for *Leadership in Higher Education*

"As with Kouzes and Posner's previous bestsellers, this work begins with personal illustrations grounded in evidence followed by strategies for converting behaviors into practice. Wisdom and leadership practices gained from this book offer invaluable leadership skills for embracing and flourishing in higher education. We look forward to purchasing copies for our colleagues across the university. This work is timely, on point, positive, solution oriented, and as always, very accessible."
—Adrian Popa, Department Chair, Gonzaga University

"Given the current era of significant change in higher education, this book is timely as a field guide, no matter what positions we are in, to make a difference in our work and impact the future of education. With specific examples from university and college leaders, it will help further support our work, both with students and with professional development for staff and faculty, in sharing best practices."
—Helen Wong, Head of Co-curricular Programs, Dean of Students' Office, Hong Kong University of Science and Technology

"What I love about this book is that it is uses everyday knowledge in an inspiring and enlightening way. When reading this book, I felt valued and inspired, even as someone who serves in an administrative role. I would encourage my colleagues and senior administration to read this book because it acknowledges our feelings about our community and environment in a way that inspires us to produce change."
—Aysen Ulupinar, Executive Assistant to the Associate Vice Chancellor, University of North Carolina at Charlotte

"Kouzes and Posner remind us that students also learn by observing those who lead and that honesty, competence, and an inspiring vision are as essential in higher education as in other domains. This book doesn't belong on a shelf—its pages should be enlarged and pinned to the walls of all college leaders who know they are always being observed by students and, as such, are always teaching leadership."
—Tom Schnaubelt, Assistant Vice Provost and Executive Director, Haas Center for Public Service, Stanford University

"I enjoyed the way Kouzes and Posner have blended theory and practice, creating something both experienced and emerging leaders will relate to easily (and retain). It is refreshing to have tangible examples from the higher education sector, demonstrating that leadership does not need to be defined as academic or professional, rather, 'of purpose and people.'"
—Clare Litten, Senior Academic Search Consultant, University of Auckland

"This is a higher education practitioners' go-to book for leadership with profound advice on dealing with the complex problems of today as well as the unknown possibilities of tomorrow."
—Clarence Green, Chief of University Police, Northwest Missouri State University

"Like every other industry, higher education is in desperate need of effective leadership—more so now than ever before. Read this book so that you can better understand how leadership actions and behaviors influence others and how you can liberate the leader within you, as well as those you work with."
—**Cheryl Johnson, Leadership Development Consultant, CAJ Leadership Consulting**

"Kouzes and Posner are applying their leadership model and insights directly to the higher education sector. Bravo! With this sector now under so much disruption, *Leadership in Higher Education* is arriving just in the nick of time. Everyone in higher education can be a leader, and everyone who works in higher education needs to read this book!"
—**Joseph Phillips, Dean, Albers School of Business and Economics, Seattle University**

"This book is relevant to all leaders in higher education, peppered with practical stories and lessons learned. I will be using this foundational book in all my Leadership in Higher Education workshops and coaching!"
—**Lillas Marie Hatala, Canadian higher education leadership development consultant**

"This book is a game changer for higher education. It's unique in that it identifies highly researched, proven leadership behaviors that provide direct data to you as to your performance as a leader. It is a very personalized and prescriptive process to becoming more effective in all aspects of your life."
—**Todd Sutherland, Chief Student Affairs Officer, Texas A&M University at Galveston**

"What I value most about Kouzes and Posner's work is their accessible and inspiring view of leadership: everyone can think of a 'personal best' leadership experience and commit to practicing behaviors that create more of them. The examples throughout this book illustrate that all of us can make exceptional things happen, regardless of our charge or position. This is vitally empowering within the hierarchical structures of higher education."
—**Abby Conover, Coordinator of Undergraduate Initiatives, Biology Teaching and Learning, University of Minnesota**

"With the challenges facing higher education today, this book could not be timelier. Kouzes and Posner provide a road map for academic administrators to become transformative leaders in the most challenging academic environment of the last half century. They have created a toolkit for academic entrepreneurs."
—**Joseph DiAngelo, Dean, Haub School of Business, Saint Joseph's University, and Past Chair, AACSB International**

"Kudos to Kouzes and Posner for continuing to demonstrate that some 'old practices' really are the best! I stuck tabs in my copy—very, very good reminders that I can never be too busy to demonstrate better leadership."
—**Elizabeth Barron Silva, Senior Assistant Dean of Finance and Administration, Santa Clara University**

"*Leadership in Higher Education* brings Kouzes and Posner's tested model into the context of higher education with tailored examples, practical suggestions, and helpful reflective questions that will get any reader thinking and more prepared to act."

—Willow Jacobson, Professor, School of Government, University of North Carolina

"While lessons and reflections on leadership from Kouzes and Posner have resonated strongly with me before, with this book those lessons are now firmly rooted in my day-to-day experience on a college campus, better equipping me for next steps in taking on new initiatives."

—Susan Dorn, Leadership Gift Officer, Bowdoin College

LEADERSHIP
IN
HIGHER
EDUCATION

LEADERSHIP

IN

HIGHER
EDUCATION

Practices That Make a Difference

JAMES M. KOUZES

AND

BARRY Z. POSNER

BK®

Berrett–Koehler Publishers, Inc.

Berrett-Koehler Publishers, Inc.
1333 Broadway, Suite 1000, Oakland, CA 94612-1921
Tel: (510) 817-2277   Fax: (510) 817-2278   www.bkconnection.com

Ordering Information

Quantity sales. Special discounts are available on quantity purchases by corporations, associations, and others. For details, contact the "Special Sales Department" at the Berrett-Koehler address above.

Individual sales. Berrett-Koehler publications are available through most bookstores. They can also be ordered directly from Berrett-Koehler: Tel: (800) 929-2929; Fax: (802) 864-7626; www.bkconnection.com.

Orders for college textbook/course adoption use. Please contact Berrett-Koehler: Tel: (800) 929-2929; Fax: (802) 864-7626.

Distributed to the U.S. trade and internationally by Penguin Random House Publisher Services.

Berrett-Koehler and the BK logo are registered trademarks of Berrett-Koehler Publishers, Inc.

The Five Practices of Exemplary Leadership is a registered trademark of James M. Kouzes and Barry Z. Posner. Used by permission.

Printed in the United States of America

Berrett-Koehler books are printed on long-lasting acid-free paper. When it is available, we choose paper that has been manufactured by environmentally responsible processes. These may include using trees grown in sustainable forests, incorporating recycled paper, minimizing chlorine in bleaching, or recycling the energy produced at the paper mill.

Library of Congress Cataloging-in-Publication Data
Names: Kouzes, James M., 1945– author. | Posner, Barry Z.
Title: Leadership in higher education : practices that make a difference /
    James M. Kouzes and Barry Z. Posner.
Description: Oakland, CA : Berrett-Koehler Publishers, [2019] | Includes
    bibliographical references and index.
Identifiers: LCCN 2019019124 | ISBN 9781523087006 (hardback)
Subjects: LCSH: Educational leadership. | Education, Higher—Aims and objectives. |
    Universities and colleges—Administration. | BISAC: EDUCATION / Leadership.
    | EDUCATION / Professional Development. | BUSINESS & ECONOMICS /
    Leadership.
Classification: LCC LB2806 .K68 2019 | DDC 378.1/01—dc23
LC record available at https://lccn.loc.gov/2019019124

First Edition
25   24   10   9   8   7   6   5   4

Cover design by Rob Johnson, Toprotype, Inc. Interior design, composition, and illustrations by Gary Palmatier, Ideas to Images. Elizabeth von Radics, copyeditor; Mike Mollett, proofreader; Paula Durbin-Westby, indexer.

Contents

v

CHAPTER **5**

Enable Others to Act

CHAPTER **6**

Encourage the Heart

CHAPTER **7**

Leadership Is Everyone's Business   137

Preface

LEADERSHIP IN HIGHER EDUCATION: *Practices That Make a Difference* is about how people on college and university campuses mobilize others to want to struggle for shared aspirations and make extraordinary things happen. It's about the behaviors that leaders use to transform values into actions, visions into realities, obstacles into innovations, segments into solidarity, and risks into rewards. It's about exercising leadership that creates the climate in which people work together to turn challenging opportunities into remarkable successes.

College and university leaders can and do make a difference in the strength of their institutions. Many, in fact, assert that leadership, more than any other single factor, will determine the future vitality of higher education.[1] Goldie Blumenstyk, a senior writer at *The Chronicle of Higher Education,* notes that "cruise-control leadership is no longer an option" and that a balance is needed between knee-jerk reactions to the latest trend and flat-footed reluctance to go after real opportunities.[2] Not only are there no shortages of challenges facing people involved in institutions of higher education but the opportunities for providing leadership within them are also available to everyone, every day.

WHO SHOULD READ THIS BOOK?

The fundamental purpose of this book is to assist people throughout the higher-education community in leading others to places they have never been before. Leadership matters whether you are a faculty member, department chair, program director, dean, vice president, or president. Likewise, leadership matters for the staff and managers of residential life, career development, student records, admissions, campus safety, information technology, library, counseling and health centers, facilities, alumni relations, development, and all other organizations on campus. We have written this book to help individuals—no matter what their position—strengthen their capacity to make extraordinary things happen. We have also written it to uplift your spirits. We have learned from our research that people in institutions of higher education are capable of developing themselves as leaders and exercising leadership far more than tradition has ever assumed possible.

This book is not about the institution or business of higher education at a macro level or about being in a leadership *position*—as if leadership were a place. It is about having the courage and spirit to make a significant difference from wherever you are within a college or university. This book is also not about leaders per se. Instead it is about the practices, behaviors, and actions associated with *leadership* and how people in higher education exercise them when making a difference.

In this book we present stories of real people from all across college campuses and university settings who achieved bigger-than-life results at their institutions. Through an analysis of their experiences, we offer practical guidance for enhancing your leadership capabilities. As you will see from the scores of examples, the principles apply regardless of the nature of your institution (e.g., public or private, secular or nonsecular, small or large, urban or rural, two-year or four-year), and they are not dependent on any particular demographic characteristic (e.g., age, gender, ethnicity, function, nationality) or personality variable. The focus is on the behaviors and actions of what people in higher education do when they are exercising exemplary leadership.

RESEARCH-BASED PRACTICES

Leadership in Higher Education is written to enhance your abilities, and the principles and practices described in it are based solidly on quantitative and qualitative research. The book has its origins in a study we began in 1983. We wanted to know what people did when they were at their "personal best" in leading others. These were experiences in which people, per their own perceptions, set their individual leadership standards of excellence. We started with an assumption that to discover best practices we didn't have to interview and survey star performers, select celebrities in academe, or people "at the top." Instead we assumed that by asking people at all levels and across a broad array of organizational settings to describe extraordinary experiences, we would be able to find and identify patterns of success. And we surely did.

The results of our initial investigation—and of the ongoing research we have conducted for nearly four decades—have been striking in their consistency and are a refutation of many leader stereotypes.[3] People frequently assume, for example, that leadership is different from one institution to the next. Nothing could be further from the truth. While each campus may look different from the outside, we find that what leaders do when they are at their best is quite similar. This pattern of behavior varies little across higher-education settings and circumstances. In the appendix we describe more fully the research basis for this book, involving a database of over 125,000 respondents and more than 100 interviews and case studies. True enough, the context keeps evolving, and the landscape of higher education has shifted over time, but leadership remains an understandable and generalizable process. Leadership is not a fad. While each leader is a unique individual, there are shared patterns to the practice of leadership.

A GUIDEBOOK ON LEADERSHIP

Think of *Leadership in Higher Education* as a guidebook to take along on your leadership journey. We have designed it to describe what leaders do, explain the fundamental principles that support these leadership practices, and provide actual case examples of real people on college and university campuses who demonstrate each practice. Based on the real-world experiences of thousands of people who have answered the call for leadership, we offer specific recommendations on what you can do to make these practices your own and to continue your development as a leader.

Chapter 1 introduces you to our point of view about leadership and briefly describes The Five Practices of Exemplary Leadership revealed in our research. In it we also describe the characteristics that people most desire in their leaders. We present the foundation on which all great leadership is built. We tell the leadership story from the inside and move outward, describing leadership first as a personal journey of exploration and then as a mobilization of others. Our research has shown that leadership is not the private reserve of a few charismatic men and women. It is a process people use when they are bringing forth the best from themselves and others. Liberate the leader in everyone, and extraordinary things happen.

In chapters 2 through 6, we explore The Five Practices, one to a chapter. The discussions are built on the results of our research, and we expand your understanding of leadership by drawing on studies of other scholars. We do not summarize the literature or all the various conceptual perspectives on leadership; instead we provide a particular point of view on leading that is empirically sound and practically valuable. We illustrate each practice with case examples, recommend actions you can take to put the practice to use, and pose questions for you to reflect on in developing your leadership capabilities. There is no sacred sequence to these chapters. We suggest that you read chapter 1 and then go wherever your interests are. Please remember though that all of these practices are essential. While you might skip around in this book, you can't skip any of the fundamentals of leadership.

In chapter 7 we discuss how leadership is a learnable set of practices, accessible to anyone. We show that leadership is everyone's business and that the first place to look for leadership is within yourself. In so doing we hope to demystify leadership and show how everyone has the capacity to lead. We discuss as well the contrasts and contradictions of leadership—no one ever said it would be easy—and how you will need to strike a balance. Finally, we offer guidance on how you can continue your growth and development, and we reveal a secret to achieving success in life.

A core theme that weaves its way through all the chapters is that *leadership is a relationship.* Whether it's one-to-one or one-to-many, leadership is a relationship between those who aspire to lead and those who choose to follow. Young or old, faculty or staff, manager or individual contributor, experienced or novice—success in leadership and success in life will continue to be a function of how well we work and get along with one another.

If you want to know more about how we conducted our research for this book, you'll find detailed information on the methodology, statistical data, and highlights of validation studies by other scholars on our website: leadershipchallenge.com. Those interested in a more thorough treatment of The Five Practices of Exemplary Leadership model and its application across a wide variety of organizational settings should read *The Leadership Challenge.*[4]

THE FUTURE OF LEADERSHIP

The domain of leaders is the future. We hope this book contributes to the ongoing revitalization of higher education, to the renewal of healthy college communities, and to greater respect and understanding among people of all traditions. We also fervently hope that it enriches your life and the lives of your students, colleagues, alumni, friends, and family. The most significant contribution leaders make is to the long-term development of people and institutions so that they can adapt, prosper, and grow.

Leadership matters not just within your university and your career. It's essential in every sector, in every community, and in every country. Right now we need more leaders, and we need them more than ever. There is so much extraordinary work to be done. We need leaders who can unite us and ignite us.

In the end we realize that leadership development is ultimately self-development. Meeting the leadership challenge is a personal—and a daily—challenge for everyone.

> James M. Kouzes
> Barry Z. Posner
> September 2019

CHAPTER 1

Leadership Is a Relationship

OGETHER WE HAVE MORE THAN 50 YEARS of experience in higher-education administration—and even more time than that research-ing and writing about how leaders make extraordinary things happen. The thousands of interviews and leadership cases we've collected, not to mention the millions of responses to our surveys, have been from people very similar to you. They're the colleagues you run into daily around campus. We've chosen to tell the stories of these everyday leaders because we firmly believe that at its core leadership is *not* about position or title. It's about caring, about relationships, and about what you *do.*

Leadership is an identifiable set of skills and practices that are available to everyone, not just a few charismatic men and women or individuals with lofty titles and positions. We challenge the myth that leadership is found only at the highest levels of an organization, whether in the halls of academe or in corporate executive suites. The theory that there are only a *few* great men and women who can lead is just plain wrong. We consider the women and men in our research to be exemplary, and so do those with whom they've worked.

We know from our experience, research, consulting, and semi-nars that everyone at your institution can learn to lead. This realization is inspiring. It gives us great hope for the future. Hope because it means that no individual, program, department, or function needs to wait around for someone to ride in on a white horse and save the day. Hope because the truth is that there is no shortage of willing people on campus searching for opportunities to make a difference.

There's another fundamental truth about leadership, one that we've known for a long time and now prize even more. In talking to campus leaders and studying their cases, we hear this unambiguous message: *leadership is a relationship*. Leadership is a relationship between those who aspire to lead and those who choose to follow.

Understanding and interacting with others is critically important in higher-education settings. Institutions of higher education are generally organized and governed according to two seemingly contradictory sets of practices—one hierarchical and the other individualistic. The most effective academic leaders know that the only way to achieve any significant change is through developing and sustaining positive working relationships.[1] Knowing people, and having trusting relationships with them, is just as essential as knowing information. Even in this nanosecond world of e-everything, this conclusion is consistent with the facts. According to the World Economic Forum's report *The Future of Jobs,* strong social and collaboration skills will be in higher demand than spectacular technical ones.[2] It's not the web of technology that matters the most; it's the web of people. Social capital, the network of relationships among people, joins intellectual and financial capital as a necessary pillar for greatness.

Success in leadership and success in life has been, is now, and will continue to be, a function of how well people work with one another. Success in leading will be wholly dependent on the capacity to build and sustain those human relationships that enable people to make extraordinary things happen on a regular basis.

THE FIVE PRACTICES OF EXEMPLARY LEADERSHIP

When we ask people to tell us about their Personal-Best Leadership Experiences—experiences that they believe are their individual standards of excellence—several significant patterns emerge. First, everyone has a story to tell. Leaders reside on every college campus, in every position and every setting. Leadership knows no racial or religious boundaries, no ethnic or cultural borders, and no age or gender constraints.

Second, when reflecting on their personal-best experiences and when listening to the leadership stories of their colleagues, people conclude that when they are at their best, the behaviors and actions of all leaders are quite similar. Regardless of the times or context, people who guide others along pioneering journeys follow surprisingly comparable paths. Though each experience is unique in its expression, there are clearly identifiable behaviors and actions that make a difference. Consequently, leadership is not about personality; it's about what you do. It's how you behave that matters—independent of the size, status, or nature of your institution; your place in the organizational hierarchy; or various demographic characteristics such as your age, gender, ethnicity, nationality, function, discipline, or length of service.

We've forged these common behaviors of what people do when they are at their personal best as leaders into a framework we call The Five Practices of Exemplary Leadership. You can think of it as a leadership operating system for how you can guide others toward peak achievements on your college or university campus. In making extraordinary things happen, leaders engage most frequently in the following five practices; they:

- Model the Way

- Inspire a Shared Vision

- Challenge the Process

- Enable Others to Act

- Encourage the Heart

The Five Practices of Exemplary Leadership—which we introduce and briefly illustrate in this chapter and will discuss extensively in later ones—aren't the private property of the people we studied or of a few select shining stars or unique personalities. They're available to anyone, in any collegiate organization or situation, who accepts the challenge of taking people and organizations to places they have never been before.

One of the greatest myths about leadership is that some people have "it" and some don't. A corollary myth is that if you don't have "it," you can't learn "it." Neither could be further from the empirical truth.[3] After reflecting on their Personal-Best Leadership Experiences, people typically come to the same conclusion as Tanvi Lotwala with the Carnegie Foundation for the Advancement of Teaching: "All of us are born leaders. We all have leadership qualities ingrained; all that we need is polishing them up and bringing them to the forefront. It is an ongoing process to develop ourselves as a leader, but unless we take on the leadership challenges presented to us on a daily basis, we cannot become better at it."

Furthermore, this leadership operating system has been widely studied and tested. Hundreds of scholars have applied The Five Practices of Exemplary Leadership framework to their investigation of leadership in higher education. From studies of college presidents,[4] business and finance officers,[5] deans and department chairs,[6] student affairs and program administrators,[7] athletic directors and coaches,[8] librarians,[9] and faculty,[10] among others, numerous scholars have found these leadership practices closely correlated with organizational and professional effectiveness.

Empirical evidence conclusively shows that those leaders in higher education who use The Five Practices most frequently have the most highly engaged and productive people in their departments and functions. According to surveys of their direct reports, exemplary leaders are more than six times more likely to employ The Five Practices in comparison with the frequency observed in the leaders of the least engaged direct reports. More specifically, the extent to which direct reports feel, for example, valued by their organizations, that they are making a difference, and that they are personally effective—all are directly related to how frequently they observe their leaders engaging in The Five Practices of Exemplary Leadership.[11]

Model the Way

Titles are granted; it's your behavior that wins you respect. This sentiment was shared across all the cases we collected. Leaders Model the Way. They know that if they want to gain commitment and achieve the highest standards, they must be models of the behaviors they expect of others. You must first be clear about your guiding principles before you can hold them up for others to emulate. Once you are clear about your core values, you can give them voice, share them with others, and act on them. "It's as straightforward," Andy Ceperley* told us, "as never asking anyone else to do something you're not willing to do yourself."

---

*The names of people quoted throughout the book are real. They are individuals we have interviewed or worked with. We've not identified their institutional affiliations for two reasons. First, some of them have or will change positions and organizations, so their affiliations would not be uniformly current. Second, because the example is meant to be about the individual—his or her actions—it should not be confused with any reputation or special circumstances associated with the institution. We've generally described the institution to give some context to the example, as well as to provide validity to the experiences (that is, generalizability) by demonstrating the breadth of college and university settings.

Andy has served in career services positions, both in the United States and abroad, experiencing a wide variety of academic institutions: public and private, secular and nonsecular, centralized and decentralized. In helping turn around one university's career center, which had experienced substantial staff turnover and burned out several directors, he explained how it was necessary for him to personally get "very deep into conversations with people across the campus." He interviewed more than 50 people and asked tons of questions, listening attentively to their perceptions of the career center. In building relationships, Andy typically began by sharing his values and beliefs about what it meant for the career center to be a service organization and his experiences about how such a center effectively engages with the campus community. He made sure to facilitate similar reflective thinking on the part of every staff member in the career center.

To effectively model the behavior they expect of others, as Andy noted, leaders must first be clear about their guiding principles. They must find their authentic voice, clearly and distinctively articulating their values. Because leaders are expected to stand up for their beliefs, they'd better have some beliefs to stand up for. By knowing what he valued most, Andy was better prepared to make decisions that were consistent with the principles he held dear. By itself, however, this isn't enough. Leaders must also make sure that what they are doing is consistent with their values and standards.

Leaders' deeds are far more important than their words when demonstrating how serious they are about what they say. Words and deeds must be consistent; if they are not, hypocrisy spreads and cynicism grows. Like Andy, leaders need to go first and set an example through daily actions that provide evidence that they are deeply committed to their beliefs. One of the best ways they prove that something is important is by demonstrating it themselves. The model that leaders set with their actions is far more powerful than anything they say. Exemplary leaders walk the talk.

Inspire a Shared Vision

People describe their Personal-Best Leadership Experiences as times when they imagined exciting and ennobling futures for their organizations. They not only envisioned what could be but also had an absolute belief in those dreams and aspirations. When they spoke about the future subsequently, their enthusiasm and energy for the vision was contagious.

Leaders have a desire to change the way things are, to create something that no one else has ever created before. In some ways leaders live their lives backward. They see pictures in their mind's eye of what the results will look like even before they've started their projects, much as architects draw blueprints or engineers build models. Their clear image of the future pulls them forward. Yet visions seen only by leaders are insufficient to effect an organized movement or a significant change. People will not follow until they accept a vision as their own. To realize the vision, you must be clear about why it is important to you, and you must be equally clear about why it should matter to those who need to share it. Therefore, leaders must be able to Inspire a Shared Vision.

Kelly McInnes started her higher-education career in admissions and worked her way up to the position of registrar, before getting hired as the director of human resources and the university's chief leadership development officer. She saw an opportunity to develop a leadership program that was specific to a Canadian public university, and she was convinced that doing so would rally people at all levels on campus. Kelly interviewed many faculty and staff administrators about their experiences and listened carefully to what they told her they were looking for, where support was available or lacking, what was working or needed fixing, and so on. She shared this feedback widely and used it to entice and recruit many academic leaders on her campus to collaborate on developing the program. Working together they co-created a program that spoke to their shared interests and aspirations.

To enlist people in a vision, leaders must know their constituents and speak their language. Similar to others we interviewed, Kelly knew that people must believe that leaders understand their needs and have their interests at heart before they will come on board. Leaders breathe life into the hopes and dreams of others and enable them to see exciting possibilities. Leaders forge a unity of purpose by showing constituents how the dream is for the common good. Leaders ignite passion in others by expressing enthusiasm for the compelling vision of their group, communicating their zeal through vivid language and an expressive style.

Challenge the Process

Leaders are pioneers—people who are willing to step out into the unknown. They search for opportunities to innovate, grow, and improve. Every single personal-best leadership case we collected involved some change from the status quo. Not one person claimed to have achieved a personal best by keeping things the same—by doing what had always or had already been done. All leaders Challenge the Process.

But leaders aren't the only creators or originators of new curricula, programs, services, or processes. In fact, it's more likely that they're not: innovation comes more from listening than from telling, from asking questions and hearing what others are thinking and have to say. When challenging the process, the leader's primary contributions are the recognition of good ideas, the support of those ideas, and the willingness to challenge the system to get new products, processes, services, and systems adopted. It might be more accurate, then, to say that leaders are *early adopters* of innovation.

J. Patrick Murphy, CM, didn't dream up the idea for a public services graduate program out of his imagination alone. He listened to the aspirations espoused by the university's president and the yearnings of many students about wanting to apply the lessons being learned in the classroom more directly in their communities. Pat also heard several of his colleagues express an interest in being involved with a program that intersected the private and public sectors and how there seemed to be opportunities to apply best practices from the for-profit sector to community-based organizations.

Pat's own dean was not initially supportive, citing financial and strategic limitations. Not easily discouraged, Pat shopped around the proposal to other parts of the campus (which at his relatively conservative university was considered a governance taboo), gaining interest and support for an interdisciplinary approach (not just in the curriculum but in staffing and funding as well). He even approached several members of the board of trustees, circled back with the president, and found sufficient support for what has now turned out to be the largest graduate program at the college.

Funding for the program was tight at the onset, as it generally is at colleges and universities, so Pat raised monies through several novel initiatives. For example, Pat and his colleagues founded a small consulting and executive training business and launched several fundraising programs, including a "pub night" to raise scholarship money for students studying in Ireland. Many of these efforts Pat had to initially bring in under the radar to keep from attracting too much attention; sometimes, he would say, "asking for forgiveness rather than permission" was necessary to learn what ideas were or were not feasible.

Leaders know well that innovation and change involve experimentation and risk. One way you can deal with these potential risks and failures is to approach change through incremental steps and small wins. Learning also unlocks the door to progress, and exemplary leaders make a point to ask, "What can we learn?" when things don't go as expected. Learning leads to little victories, which when piled on top of one another build confidence that people can meet even the most significant challenges. In so doing, leaders strengthen commitment to the long-term future.

Enable Others to Act

Grand dreams don't become significant realities through the actions of a single person. Leadership is a team effort, and to make extraordinary things happen in organizations exemplary leaders Enable Others to Act. They foster collaboration, developing relationships and building trust. Leaders engage all those who must make the project work—which was precisely the conclusion Charlie Slater reached when recounting his Personal-Best Leadership Experience of launching a new doctoral program. When asked who the leader was in developing this program, he quickly replied, "There was not a single leader but rather many leaders. At different times in the process, each one of them was critical. The program would not have come about without the leadership of all these people."

Leaders make it possible for the people around them to accomplish great things. They appreciate that those expected to produce at their most inspired levels must feel a sense of personal power and ownership. Charlie talked about how the university president, while favoring the idea, clearly understood that such an initiative couldn't successfully be launched by executive fiat, so he passed along his blessings to the dean, who in turn asked Charlie, because of his background and positive working relationships with the faculty, to accept this leadership challenge. Charlie knew that such a program could not be developed and sustained through the efforts of a single champion, and he worked with myriad faculty colleagues within the school to bring this new program to life.

This underscored for Charlie, as it did for others reflecting on their Personal-Best Leadership Experiences, the importance of commitment-and-support leadership versus the command-and-control techniques of previous generations. The work of leaders is making people feel strong, capable, and committed. Leaders enable others not by hoarding the power they have but by giving it away. The university president could not have made the program a reality by himself, and, in fact, no single person or group could have advocated successfully for the program without the cooperation of others. Working together, exemplary leaders strengthen everyone's capacity to deliver on the possibilities they imagine and the promises they make.

In the cases we analyzed, leaders like Charlie proudly discussed teamwork, collaboration, trust, and empowerment as essential elements of their efforts. People don't stick around for very long or perform at their best if their leader makes them feel weak, dependent, or alienated. But when a leader makes people feel strong and capable, raising their belief that they can do more than they ever thought possible, people will give their all. In our research it was not unusual for people to indicate that when working with their best leaders they gave to the endeavor more than 100 percent of themselves because that leader was able to elicit from them more than what they themselves had thought possible. When leadership is a relationship founded on trust and confidence, people take risks, make changes, and keep organizations and movements alive.

Encourage the Heart

The climb to the top of any endeavor is arduous and steep, and it is altogether easy for people to become exhausted, frustrated, and disenchanted. Leaders Encourage the Heart of their constituents to carry on, to continue even when they might be tempted to give up. Genuine acts of caring, whether exhibited in dramatic gestures or simple actions—for example, bringing food to a sick colleague, visiting people in the hospital, or sending a handwritten note of appreciation—uplift the spirits and draw people forward. Jennifer Dirking, associate director for her community college's foundation, says that she is always on the lookout for ways to foster a climate in which "people feel cared about and genuinely appreciated."

An award for the "most outstanding faculty member" used to be given each year at Barry Posner's school. In those days he was a faculty member and said that he "could never understand how there could be one award, with so many disciplines, and, given each discipline's different standards, how the faculty and dean's office could decide on what 'most outstanding' meant." So, when he became dean, Barry says,

> I was determined we'd change the system and do more to recognize the excellence among our *many* faculty colleagues. Working with our Council of Department Chairs, we established a specific set of accomplishments, from unsatisfactory to exemplary, which were appropriate to all disciplines and all ranks. Any faculty member who could be exemplary in teaching and scholarship and service would certainly be, in any of our minds, "extraordinary"—and that's what we called the award. We could all be proud when anyone in the school was extraordinary.

In the first year, six Extraordinary Faculty Awards were given. Five years later 13 were awarded. As Barry recalls, "I thought it was great that the standards hadn't changed, but the behavior—and hence the performance—of our faculty had risen to the ideal we set. With this change in criteria for the award, we took a giant step in eliminating competition among ourselves for 'who's the best' and rather collectively focused on what everyone needed to do to be at their best."

It is part of the leader's job to show appreciation for people's contributions and to create a culture of celebration. Over the years we've seen thousands of examples of individual recognition and group celebration, from handwritten thank-you notes to marching bands and "This Is Your Life" ceremonies. Yet recognition and celebration aren't merely about fun and games, though both abound when leaders Encourage the Hearts of their constituents. Neither are they about pretentious ceremonies designed to present some artificial sense of camaraderie. Encouragement is curiously serious business. It's how leaders visibly and behaviorally link rewards with performance.

When striving to raise quality standards, recover from a disaster, or make a dramatic change of any kind, leaders make sure that people see the benefits of aligning behavior with cherished values. And leaders also know that celebrations and rituals, when done with authenticity and from the heart, build a strong sense of collective identity and community spirit that can carry a group through tough times.

THE OTHER SIDE OF THE LEADERSHIP STORY

A fundamental truth that weaves itself throughout all Personal-Best Leadership Experiences is that they are never stories about solo performances. Leaders never make extraordinary things happen all by themselves. Leaders mobilize *others* to want to struggle for shared aspirations. As we have already said, leadership is a relationship between those who aspire to lead and those who choose to follow. You can't have one without the other.

To lead effectively, you have to appreciate the underlying dynamics of the leader-constituent relationship.[12] A leader-constituent relationship characterized by fear and distrust will never produce anything of lasting value. A relationship characterized by mutual respect and confidence will overcome the greatest adversities and leave a legacy of significance. Any discussion of leadership must attend to the dynamics of this relationship. Strategies, tactics, skills, and techniques are futile without an understanding of the essential human aspirations that connect people with their leaders and leaders with their people.

To balance our understanding of leadership, for nearly four decades we have conducted surveys about the personal values, traits, and characteristics that people indicate are most important to them in an individual they would willingly follow. A key word in this sentence is *willingly*. It is one thing to follow someone because you think you have to "or else," and it's quite another when you follow an individual because you *want to*.

What sort of person would you listen to, take advice from, be influenced by, and willingly follow, not because you have to but because you want to? What does it take for you to be the kind of person whom others want to follow, doing so enthusiastically and voluntarily? Understanding and responding to these expectations is essential to the exercise of exemplary leadership.

What People Look For in Their Leaders

Responses from more than 100,000 respondents—in higher education as well as in every industry and scores of countries around the globe—affirm and enrich the picture that emerged from our studies of personal bests. The survey results have been striking in their consistency over the years.[13] Our evidence shows that a person must pass several essential character tests before they earn the designation *leader* from other people, as demonstrated by the data presented in figure 1.1.

All the characteristics receive votes, and therefore each one is important to some individuals. What is both most striking and evident, however, is that over time and across continents *only four* have continuously received the majority (more than 60 percent) of the preferences. What people *most* look for and admire in a leader has been constant. If people are going to follow someone *willingly*, they must believe the individual is honest, competent, inspiring, and forward-looking. Indeed, from the opposite perspective, ask yourself how willing you would be to follow someone who was dishonest, incompetent, uninspiring, and lost! Not very likely, right?

Responses from hundreds of faculty members—many of whom are department chairs, associate deans, and deans—over the past few years reaffirm these findings. Answers from student personnel administrators, registrars, admissions counselors, development staff, public safety officers, and recreation and athletic directors are strikingly similar to those from faculty. Students also indicate that these top four characteristics—honest, competent, inspiring, and

84% **Honest**
Truthful, has integrity, trustworthy, has character, ethical

66% **Competent**
Capable, proficient, effective, gets job done, professional

66% **Inspiring**
Uplifting, enthusiastic, energetic, humorous, cheerful, optimistic, positive about the future

62% **Forward-looking**
Visionary, foresighted, concerned about the future, has a sense of direction

47% **Intelligent**
Bright, smart, thoughtful, intellectual, reflective, logical

40% **Broad-minded**
Open-minded, flexible, receptive, tolerant

39% **Dependable**
Reliable, conscientious, responsible

37% **Supportive**
Helpful, offers assistance, comforting

35% **Fair-minded**
Just, unprejudiced, objective, forgiving

32% **Straightforward**
Direct, candid, forthright

31% **Cooperative**
Collaborative, team player, responsive

28% **Ambitious**
Aspiring, hardworking, striving

23% **Caring**
Appreciative, compassionate, concerned, loving, nurturing

22% **Determined**
Dedicated, resolute, persistent, purposeful

22% **Courageous**
Bold, daring, gutsy

18% **Loyal**
Faithful, dutiful, unswerving in allegiance, devoted

17% **Imaginative**
Creative, innovative, curious

17% **Mature**
Experienced, wise, has depth

10% **Self-controlled**
Restrained, self-disciplined

5% **Independent**
Self-reliant, self-sufficient, self-confident

Figure 1.1 Personal values, traits, and characteristics that people look for in their leaders. Note that several synonyms were included in each category. The percentages represent respondents from six continents: Africa, Asia, Australia, Europe, North America, and South America. The majority are from the United States. Because we asked people to select seven characteristics, the total adds up to about 700 percent.

forward-looking—are most highly valued in their very best teachers. Studies show that these four characteristics do not significantly vary across industries, cultures, nationalities, and organizational functions and hierarchies or by gender, ethnicity, level of education, or age.[14]

These investigations of the characteristics of admired leaders reveal consistent patterns with the stories we learned from people telling us about their Personal-Best Leadership Experiences. The Five Practices of Exemplary Leadership and the characteristics of admired leaders are complementary perspectives on the same subject. When they're performing at their peak, leaders are doing more than just getting results. They're also responding to the expectations of the people they are working with, underscoring the point that leadership is a relationship and that the relationship is one of service to a purpose and to other people.

You'll see in more detail how exemplary leaders respond to the needs of their constituents as we weave these personal characteristics of being honest, competent, inspiring, and forward-looking into the text of the subsequent chapters on the leadership practices. For example, being regarded as honest is essential if you are going to Model the Way. The leadership practice of Inspire a Shared Vision requires your being forward-looking and inspiring. When leaders Challenge the Process, they enhance the perception that they're dynamic and concerned about the future. *Trustworthiness,* a synonym for *honesty,* implies that you have others' best interests at heart and is an essential component in both why and how leaders Enable Others to Act. In recognizing and celebrating notable contributions and accomplishments—that is, Encourage the Heart—you strengthen people's commitment to shared values and underscore how collaborating is aligned with achieving the vision. When leaders demonstrate capacity in all of The Five Practices, they show others that they have the competence to make extraordinary things happen.

CREDIBILITY IS THE FOUNDATION OF LEADERSHIP

While the fact that what people look for in their leaders has remained consistent over time, despite the ever-shifting forces affecting higher education, there is another profound implication revealed by this descriptive data. These survey results have a solid conceptual foundation in what social psychologists and communication experts refer to as "credibility." In assessing such questions as why some people are more believable than others, how reputations are formed, what constitutes opinion leaders, or what factors create role models, researchers have demonstrated that the key dimensions of credibility are remarkably similar to the four characteristics people most desire in their leaders.[15]

If you are going to ask others to follow you to some uncertain future—a future that may not be realized in their tenure or even their lifetime—and if the journey is going to require hardships and possibly sacrifices, it is imperative that people believe in you, the person they will be following. The countless programs to develop leaders, the courses and classes, the books and CDs, the blogs and websites offering tips and techniques—all are meaningless unless the people who are supposed to be following believe in the person who's supposed to be leading. The bottom line is that more than anything *people want leaders who are credible.*

People must be able to believe in their leaders—that her words can be trusted, that he will do what he says, that she is personally excited and enthusiastic about the direction in which the group is headed, and that he has the knowledge and skills to lead. This is the First Law of Leadership: *If people don't believe in the messenger, they won't believe the message.*

What does it take to "believe in the messenger" and be viewed as credible? When we ask people, "What does credibility look like in action? How do you know if someone is credible?" their answers do not vary by the nature of their institution or by what they do or even by who they are (e.g., age, gender, ethnicity, faculty, staff). These are the most common phrases people use to describe the behaviors and actions of people who are credible:

- "They practice what they preach."

- "They walk the talk."

- "Their actions are consistent with their words."

- "They put their money where their mouth is."

- "They follow through on their promises."

- *"They do what they say they will do."*

That last response is the most frequent. When it comes to deciding whether a leader is believable, people first listen to the words, then they watch the actions. A judgment of "credible" is handed down when words and deeds are consonant. If people don't see consistency—if, for instance, special favors are alleged around admissions, popular or favorite students aren't disciplined for honor codes violations, misconduct by alumni donors is overlooked, staff are maligned, colleagues are denigrated—they conclude that the leader is, at best, not really serious or, at worst, an outright hypocrite. When leaders do practice what they preach—and do so consistently—people are more willing to entrust them with their careers, their security, and their future.

This realization leads to a straightforward prescription for establishing credibility: *DWYSYWD*, or *Do What You Say You Will Do*. This commonsense definition of credibility corresponds directly to the leadership practice of Model the Way. To Model the Way and be credible in action, you must be clear about your beliefs; you must know what you stand for. That's the *say* part of DWYSYWD. Then you must put what you say into practice: you must act on your beliefs and *do*.

It is when leaders' words and deeds match up that people see them as believable and credible. To be authentic, to gain and sustain the moral authority to lead, is essential to the practice of Model the Way.

Because of this important connection between words and actions, we begin discussing The Five Practices with a thorough examination of the principles and behaviors that bring Model the Way to life. In the chapters that follow, we introduce you to people at colleges and universities who put the five leadership practices into action and made extraordinary things happen within their institutions.

CHAPTER 2

Model the Way

Tonya Nilsson, a senior lecturer in the civil engineering department, recalls that her mother, who was a manager at a local library, would often remark that "she would never ask her employees to do something she wouldn't be willing to do herself." This mantra is firmly ingrained in Tonya, who feels that it isn't right for her "to judge someone for being an ineffective teacher and for being unwilling to step it up if I am not willing to model better teaching myself." This is just one of the reasons why Tonya routinely equips herself with various teaching tools to better engage with her students and participates in university committees focused on improving student learning. In these venues she shares her values and beliefs with colleagues and encourages them to use more-effective teaching methods. She believes that all teachers are leaders who should not restrict themselves to merely managing content delivery but should also be nurturing and prepare the next generation of engineers and scientists.

Tonya makes sure that she aligns her values and actions in her own classroom. For example, she believes that one way teachers demonstrate respect for their students is by starting class on time. She makes it clear at the onset of her courses that being late for class is unacceptable. She holds quizzes at the very beginning of class to make the point that being late can have negative consequences. She follows this up in her own actions by indicating that she'll give students extra points if *she* is ever tardy.

Tonya also believes that it is imperative that engineers communicate well because doing so not only ensures safety but also maintains project progress. She stresses the development of communication skills and demonstrates the same in her lectures. She begins class with an agenda or overview, informing students of her learning objectives and what she is going to cover. She takes care to ensure that her board notes are legible and clearly stated and that problem-solution handouts are easy to understand. "Everything I do must be clear long after the class session is over," she says.

Leaders like Tonya understand that they must fully comprehend the values, beliefs, and assumptions that drive them. They have to freely and honestly choose the principles they will use to guide their actions. Before you can clearly communicate your message, you must be clear about the message you want to deliver. And before you can *do* what you say, you must be sure that you *mean* what you say.

Words themselves, however, aren't enough, no matter how noble. You must find *your* voice and authentically communicate your beliefs in ways that uniquely represent who you are so that others recognize that you're the one who's speaking and not someone else. "Above all else, academic deans—and all leaders—must come to terms with themselves," explains Deryl Leaming, former dean and the author of several books on academic leadership. "They must understand their own inclinations and motivations and be comfortable with who they are."[1]

The most effective leaders in higher education are those who most frequently Model the Way. We asked direct reports how often their leaders engaged in the six behaviors associated with Model the Way on the *Leadership Practices Inventory* (LPI), with assessments ranging from 1 (Almost never) to 10 (Almost always). We also asked them a separate question about the extent to which they agreed or disagreed with the statement *Overall, this person is an effective leader* (1 = Strongly disagree and 5 = Strongly agree). The analysis showed that the effectiveness ratings of leaders by their direct reports increased systematically ($p < 0.001$) as leaders were observed engaging more and more frequently in the behaviors associated with modeling the way. There was a 63 percent bump in effectiveness from the bottom to the top quartile.

CLARIFY YOUR VALUES

What stands out when we ask people to think about the historical leaders they most admire *and* could imagine following is that they chose individuals with strong beliefs about matters of principle. The leaders most often named all had an unwavering commitment to a clear set of values. They were all passionate about their causes. They were self-assured and comfortable with who they were. The lesson is unmistakable: becoming a leader people would willingly follow requires being a person of principle. "The simple truth is that we cannot be leaders," Deryl explains, "unless others look up to and want to follow us, and the likelihood of that happening when we are insecure in who we are is remote."[2]

People expect their leaders to speak out on matters of values and conscience. But you can't speak out if you don't know what is important to you, what you care about deeply. To speak effectively, you must find your authentic voice. Earning and sustaining personal credibility requires that you can clearly articulate your deeply held beliefs.

Lillas Marie Hatala had a successful career as a human resource development manager at a large Canadian retailer, but she was seeking a more meaningful way to work with people. "I wanted to make a difference," says Lillas, "in the lives of leaders and their constituents in the educational workplace." She was recruited to start-up operations as director of business and leadership programs for a large public university.

Like any new leader, Lillas realized that she "had to earn credibility. In any organization, credibility building is a process that takes time, hard work, devotion, and patience." Additionally, she realized that coming in as an outsider to higher education can be especially trying because there's some skepticism about intentions and the transferability of competencies. This was even truer in her case because one of her initial projects was a leadership development program for department chairs. Imagine their rumblings: *How can someone from retail possibly help develop the skills of those in academia?*

"In the early years," Lillas says, "some naysayers scoffed at my work, saying, 'You're talking about business, and this is a university,' or 'You can't herd cats,' or 'Watch the fluff,' and so on. Painful as some of this was at the time, it not only contributed to my challenge but it caused me to persevere....It reinforced my intent to contribute to developing a more encouraging and nurturing culture than what I was experiencing."

Throughout this challenging project, Lillas turned to a simple method to aid her in staying the course. Every day she used personal journal writing for reflection and contemplation. "I use my journal to dialogue with the small still voice within," she says. "Every evening I'd ask, *What have I done today that demonstrates this value that is near and dear to me? What have I done inadvertently to demonstrate that this is not a value to me? What do I need to do more of to more fully express my values?*" By daily clarifying and reaffirming her values, Lillas was able to strengthen her resolve to make a difference in the institution's culture and the way that people related to and respected one another.

As Lillas's story illustrates, values are your guides, your personal bottom line. They equip you with a moral compass by which to navigate the course of your daily life. Clarity of values is essential to discerning which way is north, south, east, and west. The clearer you are, the easier it is to stay on the path you've chosen. You especially need this kind of guidance in difficult and uncertain times. When there are daily challenges that can throw you off course, it's crucial that you have some signposts that tell you where you are and keep you on track.

Values also serve as guides to action. They inform your decisions on what to do and what not to do, as well as when to say yes or no and understand *why* you mean it. If you believe, for instance, that heated debate can stimulate thinking and creativity, you should know what to do if people with differing views keep getting cut off when they offer up a fresh idea. If you value collaboration over individualistic achievement, you'll know what to do when your most experienced career center adviser skips team meetings and refuses to share information with colleagues. If you value independence and initiative over conformity and obedience, you'll be more likely to speak up and challenge a policy when you think it's wrong.

As the data in figure 2.1 shows, there is a dramatic relationship between how people rate the effectiveness of their leaders and the

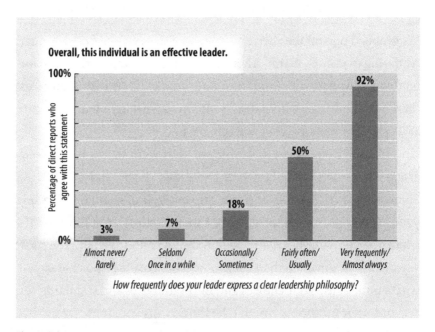

Figure 2.1 The effectiveness ratings of leaders increase systematically with the extent that they are seen as having a clear leadership philosophy.

extent to which they find them clear about their leadership philosophy. Only 3 percent of people rate as effective those leaders who are viewed as almost never/rarely being clear about their personal leadership philosophy; the effectiveness percentage goes up by a factor of more than 30 for those leaders reported as very frequently/almost always clear about their leadership philosophy.

Explore Your Inner Territory

We were talking about where leadership begins, and our conversation went something like this:

> *Jim:* I think leadership begins with discontent. You are dissatisfied with the status quo, the ways things are currently going.
>
> *Barry:* True enough, but that's too dismal a view for me. I think leadership actually begins with caring. What do you care enough about to see if it could be any better?
>
> *Jim:* Okay, then, let's look up the word *caring* in the dictionary.

We grabbed one off the shelf and opened it to *care.* The first meaning: "suffering of mind: GRIEF." There it was. Suffering and caring, discontent and concern—all come from one source. Deep within all of us, there is something we hold dear, something we'll fight hard to secure and celebrate joyfully when we achieve it.

In time we realized that what we both were saying is that *leadership begins with something that grabs hold of you and won't let go.* Something isn't working, and you care enough to change it. Finding your voice requires exploring your inner territory. You have to take a journey into your heart and soul to discover your values. You must wrestle with them enough to determine what's really important to you, what's underlying your choices and the boundaries and standards you set, and what motivates you to take the actions you do.

You *must* know what you care about. You can be authentic only when you lead others according to the principles that matter most to you. Otherwise you're just putting on an act. If you don't care, how can you expect others to do so? If you don't burn with desire to be true to something you hold passionately, how can you expect that commitment from others? And until you get close enough to the flame to feel the heat, how can you know the source?

The fact is that the first person who must follow you is you! To lead others you first have to believe in yourself. If you do not, others will not believe in you or have confidence in you and consequently will not willingly follow your lead.[3] One staff member told us that she could seldom, as she put it, "get on board" with her supervisor because she found it impossible to know what he stood for: "I was unsure about what he really felt was important and hesitant to follow his suggestions." The counterpoint to this observation, as voiced by an incoming department chair, was his realization that "any changes I wished to see in the faculty or staff needed to start with me, as I am their example. If whatever I'm trying to implement I don't believe in first, why should my colleagues? If I don't demonstrate the values I am expecting from others, why should they follow me or those values?"

Alan Glassman had to explore such questions himself when he accepted the university president's request that he lead the institution's first strategic-planning process after a natural disaster had destroyed much of the campus. Why did Alan accept this invitation, especially after several "highly paid and well-credentialed" external consultants had been dismissed from the project? Alan explained that he stepped up to the challenge because he felt that he "wanted to give something back to a campus that had supported me very well during my career." Additionally, it was a chance, he said, for him to participate and see firsthand the creation and development of "a high-involvement framework for organizational change," which he had been teaching about for several years in his classes.

This experience would test both his belief system and how well he could model his expectations. He designed a high-involvement process that offered faculty and staff the opportunity to "create the future" for the institution. By appealing to people's desire to give back to the campus, Alan "created space for volunteers to come forward, offer their services and perspectives." The process confirmed one of Alan's most deeply held values: given a chance, people will contribute and do the right thing.

Like Alan, people discovered from their Personal-Best Leadership Experiences that becoming a credible leader requires learning how to express yourself in ways that are uniquely your own. You cannot lead through someone else's values, someone else's words. You cannot lead out of someone else's experience. You can lead only out of your own. Unless it's your style, your words, it's not you; it's an abstraction.

It's one thing to give voice to your words; it's another to give voice in tune and with a personal style. If you're not the genuine article, can you expect others to respect you? People don't follow your technique. They follow *you*—your message and your embodiment of that message. To be a leader, you must confront this central issue for yourself. You don't have to copy someone else, you don't have to read a script written by someone else, and you don't have to wear someone else's fashions. Instead you are free to choose what you want to express and the way you want to express it. We'd argue that you have a responsibility to your constituents to express yourself in a singular manner—in a way they would immediately recognize as yours. Researchers have consistently demonstrated a significant relationship between a leader's clarity and commitment to a set of core values and their likelihood of being successful.[4]

Build and Affirm Shared Values

Clarity about personal values is an essential part of finding your voice. Leaders don't stand up for just some personal or idiosyncratic values. In the process of setting an example, leaders endeavor to lead their constituents from what *I* believe to what *we* believe. In other words:

Do What We Say We Will Do. A leader's promise is really an organization's promise, regardless of whether the organization is a team of two, a department of 15, a program involving several hundred, or a school of many thousand.

Nicole Matouk was a student records analyst in the law school when the university implemented a major transition from the semester to the quarter system. Because of all the necessary preparations in advance of the change—for example, overhauling the computer systems—and because of the quarter system itself, which required an additional term of work, by the end of the school year everyone was exhausted and in need of encouragement. The associate dean sent an email to the people working in the registrar's office, asking for their feedback about the transition and inviting them to meet with her over coffee and talk informally about the transition process.

Everyone had the opportunity to address the topics they felt strongly about, and all had equal and ample time to express themselves. No one felt pressured, and the staff felt free to voice their opinions without fear of retribution. The associate dean asked directly about what things they could do to provide students with faster and more accurate answers and to give students an enhanced, more hassle-free experience. Nicole commented that "not only did the associate dean's questions keep us from taking a bath in the negative emotions we were feeling but they helped us refocus on our goals as an office." Some of the dean's questions had to do with making their jobs more efficient; others dealt with new systems that could be implemented to make procedures easier for both the students and the staff.

Nicole went on to explain:

> She used these questions to affirm our shared values. She didn't have to struggle to think of the questions she wanted to ask or how she would connect what we were discussing to our goals; her values were guiding her questions. As we talked I could tell she was leading me in a certain direction, but it didn't seem manipulative. This was so much more powerful to me than reading about

the values in the handbook. I was generating the answers to her questions, so I felt this is what I believe, not just what I am supposed to agree with. Not only did this meeting help our team individually generate answers that were in line with our values and the office's values but it also helped us affirm our shared values as an office. We came out of that meeting more united and with the knowledge that we were all working to achieve the same thing instead of pulling against each other for time and attention.

Nicole's experience reaffirms that people are more loyal and committed when they believe that their values and those of the organization are aligned. They can be more creative and engaged because they become immersed in what they are doing. The quality and accuracy of communication and the integrity of the decision-making process increase when people across the campus feel that they share common values.

Discovering and affirming shared values is the foundation for building productive and genuine work relationships. While credible leaders honor the diversity of their many constituencies, they also stress their common values. Leaders build on agreement. They don't try to get everyone to be in accord on everything—this goal is unrealistic, perhaps even impossible. Moreover, to achieve it would negate the very advantages of diversity. But to take the first step, then a second, and then a third, people must have some common core of understanding. If disagreements over fundamental values persist, the result is intense conflict, false expectations, and diminished capacity.

Recognition of institutional values that everyone can embrace provides the campus community with a common language and framework for communicating the premise for making key decisions. Research clearly shows that alignment of individual, group, and institutional values generates tremendous energy.[5] Agreement intensifies commitment, enthusiasm, and drive; individuals have reasons for caring about their work. When people can care about what they are doing, they are more effective and satisfied. They experience less stress and tension. Shared values are the internal compasses that enable people to act both independently and interdependently.[6]

Important as it is that leaders forthrightly articulate the principles for which they stand, what leaders say and do must be consistent with the aspirations of their constituents. When university administrators, at whatever level, advocate or speak out about values that aren't representative of the collective will, they are ineffective at mobilizing people to act as one. Leaders set an example for all of their constituents based on a shared understanding of what is expected. This means they have gained consensus on a common cause and a collective set of principles. This gives them legitimacy in building and affirming a community of shared values.

Renew Shared Values

Periodically taking the institution's pulse on the clarity of and consensus around values is well worthwhile. Whether through surveys, forums, town hall gatherings, coffee chats, webinars, or other methods, the process of assessing current sentiment engages the entire campus community in discussing values and helps ensure that they are inclusive of an ever-changing constituency. Once people are clear about their leaders' values, about their own values, and about shared values, they know what's expected of them. They are better able to handle higher levels of uncertainty and ambiguity, and they can better deal with any conflicting demands between work and their personal lives.

But questions such as *What are our basic principles?* and *What do we believe in?* are far from simple. Even with explicitly stated common values, there may be little agreement on the meaning of each statement of belief. At our own institution, not an academic year goes by without everyone—or at least some significant portion of the campus—getting engaged in discussions about core institutional values. We talk regularly about such core principles as "educating for competence, conscience, and compassion" and determining what it means to be a "Jesuit, Catholic" university. A common understanding of values comes about through that dialogue; it emerges from a *process,* not a pronouncement. Leaders must engage their constituents in conversations about values issues. After all, if there's no agreement about values, what exactly is the leader—and everyone else—going to model?

Shared values must be more than campus or program advertising slogans. They must be genuinely supported and broadly endorsed. Faculty and staff must be able not only to enumerate the values but also to provide relatively common interpretations of how those values are put into practice. They must know how the values influence the way they teach, address issues, recruit faculty, hold ceremonies, provide services to students and alumni, and so on. They must also know how these values contribute directly to making their college or university unique and distinctive.

Shared values emerge from listening, appreciating, and building consensus. We observed one student union director who spent his first months going around both the building and the campus, talking with people. He listened as people told him about what was working and what needed improvement or fixing. In these conversations he also had an opportunity to share information about himself, his values, and his experiences on other campuses. When changes were made, he referenced them against much of what he had heard in these conversations, and people could tell that he had been true to his promise to listen and be responsive.

For people on campus and within various departments and programs to understand the values and come to agree with them, they must participate in the process. A unified voice on values results from discovery and dialogue: unity is forged, not forced. You must provide a chance for people within your department, program, or unit to engage in a discussion of what the values mean and how their personal beliefs and behaviors are influenced by what the institution stands for.

You must also be prepared to discuss values and expectations in the recruitment, selection, and orientation of new people to your team, department, or program. On this exact point, a research center Fellow lamented that "values are, unfortunately, often communicated very poorly, not just in academia. They become another item to check off the list, along with how to fill out forms for parking, selecting health-care options, and where to get office supplies. With so many tasks to accomplish, discussion of values and beliefs often falls by the wayside." He believed that values "cannot be defined and then set aside to gather dust. They need to be lived and their importance demonstrated overtly in decisions."

LEAD BY EXAMPLE

Leaders *enact* the meaning of the organization in every decision they make and in every step they take toward the future they envision. Leaders understand that they bring shared values to life in a variety of settings—in weekly department meetings, one-on-one conferences, donor telephone calls, faculty and staff council sessions, and visits with alumni, vendors, suppliers, and community members. For example, the data in figure 2.2 shows that the more often leaders are observed setting a personal example of what they expect of others, the more their direct reports indicate that they trust management.

How you spend your time, how you react to critical incidents, the stories you tell, the questions you ask, and the language you use—all are leadership tools for setting an example. How you apply these tools should not be haphazard and left to chance. Although serendipity may play a role, you must continuously be on the lookout for ways to establish yourself as a leader by demonstrating how core beliefs shape and govern your actions.

Modeling the way may appear rather basic and obvious, but it's all in the attention and the doing. Each tool enables you to make a

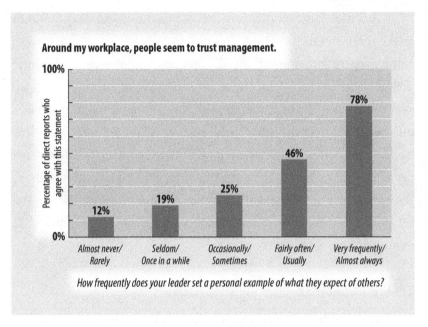

Figure 2.2 Setting a personal example of what leaders expect from others increases the extent to which people trust them.

conscious commitment to a shared way of being visible and tangible to others. Conscientious application of these tools can often challenge aspiring leaders, but failure to use them will foster cynicism. It's always useful to keep in mind that sometimes the longest distance you have to travel is the distance from your mouth to your feet, from what you say to what you do.

Spend Time and Pay Attention

How you spend your time is the single clearest indicator, especially to others, of what's important to you. What do you say is your top priority? Whether it's faculty, students, staff, or alumni, the question is, *How much of your daily time do you spend with them?* When Jeanne O'Laughlin, OP, was president of a small religious university, her vision was to create a caring environment on campus. To back that up, she routinely stopped and talked with students she met as she walked across campus. The first day on the job, another college president pedaled to work on an old bicycle and chained it to the sign that said "President's Car"—providing a simple statement about the values of sustainability and frugality.

Leaders make obvious connections between how they allocate their time and what they consider to be their priorities and core values. What does it mean when the provost comes to a meeting of the student senate or conducts a meeting with students in the administration building versus the student union? What signal does it send when the vice president for business services comes to a school's faculty meeting to discuss the budget rather than sending a budget analyst? If you say alumni are important, how much time goes by without meeting with them? If you say students are important, when's the last time you sat in on a class, attended a student presentation, or joined in a student-sponsored event?

Setting an example often means arriving early, staying late, and being there to show you care. Faculty members who show up early to their classes and linger afterward to answer questions and chat with students successfully communicate their own and their institution's commitment to caring about students. Learning the names and areas of study and interest of the students who work in your office sets an example of how people should be treated—and valued—in the workplace, even if they are part-time or temporary.

Calendars never lie when it comes to sending a message to others about how you prioritize your time and how this allocation aligns with your values and priorities—or not. Time, obviously, is a finite quantity, so make sure your distribution of it is in synch with where and what you want people to pay attention to. Don't be too busy to take a moment to chat and get to know the people who work with, and around, you.

Turn Critical Incidents into Teachable Moments

Choosing to spend time on core values is essential in sending the signal that you're serious about an issue. But even the most disciplined leaders can't stop the intrusion of the unexpected. There are constant interruptions, brief interactions, and extraordinary variety in everyday life on a college campus. Critical incidents—chance occurrences, particularly at a time of stress and challenge—offer significant moments of learning for leaders and constituents. Critical incidents present opportunities for leaders to teach valuable lessons about appropriate norms of behavior.

Jim Lyons, dean of students, was always on the lookout for critical incidents that he called "teachable moments" for the campus. These were the times that something unexpected happened, usually (but not always) negative, and campus administrators had a leadership choice to make about how they wanted to frame and respond to the incident.

For example, when a violation of the university's honor code occurs (as it will inevitably), is the focus narrowly on dealing with students caught cheating or is it more broadly focused on bringing the entire campus community (students, faculty, and staff) into a discussion of what it means to have, and live by, an honor code? What does it mean to be responsible and accountable not just for your behavior but also for how others behave? Incidents will happen, and the question for leaders is more than what the punishment will be. It's bigger than that. It's about the lessons they want to teach as a result of their response. Housing departments and programs, for example, have moved from simply penalizing people for breaking the rules to encouraging people to follow the rules determined by the residents themselves—these "rules" then represent the shared values of the community.

Critical incidents are those events in leaders' lives that offer the chance to improvise while still staying true to the script. Although they can't be explicitly planned, it's useful to keep in mind that the way you handle such incidents—how you link actions and decisions to shared values—says volumes about what's important.

For example, some deans and departments make it a big deal when a faculty member's book receives an award, and others don't. One university advancement officer vigorously rings a bell, located in the center of the office, and calls everyone together whenever anyone successfully solicits a donation over a certain amount; many just take such accomplishments for granted. Some athletic directors make a personal appearance in the team's locker room after a narrow overtime defeat to remind the players about being proud to play at their best in spite of the scoreboard. After a particularly disturbing racial incident, the campus police chief made a personal appearance at a meeting of the student senate to talk about such tensions and the need to reach out and ensure the safety of each person (students, faculty, and staff) on campus. He also held individual discussions with each public safety officer, over three shifts, to share similar beliefs and to learn about their concerns.

Tell Stories to Teach Virtues

Critical incidents are often the most dramatic sources of moral lessons about how people should and should not behave. They become stories to pass along, whether around the classrooms and residence halls; among faculty, staff, and students; or even from generation to generation. To understand the teaching power of stories, all you have to do is listen to the tales that alumni relate when they are together during homecoming events:

- The story about an administrative assistant who enabled them to graduate on time by approving their petition to add a class after the enrollment deadline

- The faculty member who made a point of coming to their volleyball games, visibly cheering, and talking about how they

played when they came to class or bumped into each other in
the student union

- The counseling center director who always made time in
  his schedule to speak with them whenever they were feeling
  stressed-out

- The department chair who found the resources to send them
  to an overseas (expensive!) conference, which enabled them to
  make connections with colleagues that otherwise would not
  have been possible

- The residence hall director who spent hours listening to them
  complain about a roommate and eventually helped them find a
  better place to live

While the leader's message is vital, and how it is framed is critical, the
process by which it is communicated is just as significant. Stories can
serve as mental maps that help people make the connection between
what is important—the purpose and values—and how to put those
things into practice. When people hear a story about how someone
like themselves enacted a value, they are more likely to see themselves
doing the same.

Judith Ramaley, a former biology professor and university president, suggests that aspiring leaders can become good storytellers by
inviting members of their college community to tell them about the
good things that are happening and what they believe contributes to
the quality of the institution. Armed with this material, she says, "you
can be a storyteller...and your stories will help create meaning and
direction for the institution."[7]

When a leader is trying to communicate the values of an organization, what would have more of an impact: a policy statement that
says "Thou shalt establish personal relationships with alumni" or a
story about the dean attending the Alumni Association's monthly

TGIFs? Similarly, what would be more persuasive: seeing statistics about how much stress students experience while at college or hearing a story about a student on your campus—who might have been in your class or worked in your office—who had committed suicide? If you said the story, your answer is consistent with the data. In fact, information is more quickly and accurately remembered when it is first presented in the form of an example or a story, especially compared with facts, figures, and formal policy pronouncements.[8] Stories are far better able to accomplish the objectives of teaching, mobilizing, and motivating than bullet points on an overhead. Well-told stories reach inside people and pull them along. They give everyone the sense of being there and of learning what is really important about the experience.

Choose Words and Questions Deliberately

It's been said that people are "prisoners" of their organizational vocabulary.[9] If you disagree, try talking about the personnel in your college or university for even a day without using the words *employee, manager, boss, supervisor, staff, subordinate,* or *hierarchy.* We've all come to accept certain words as the reality of organizational life. Those words can trap you into a particular way of thinking about your roles and relationships.

Leaders understand the power of words and are attentive to language. The words we choose to use are metaphors for concepts that define attitudes and behaviors, structures and systems. Our words evoke images of what we hope to accomplish and how we expect people to behave. Too often on college campuses, some people hold tightly to designations that set them apart—and frequently above—others. Such distinctions make it challenging to find common ground.

Consider the simple shift in language and meaning when the vernacular *extracurricular*—describing those activities on campus directed by the student affairs divisions—was dropped in favor of *co-curricular,* recognizing the holistic notion of the educational and learning process on campus. The shift in thinking on college campuses from building "dormitories" to establishing "residential learning communities" is another effort in this same direction. This shift in language changes how many staff members and faculty understand the role they play on campus in the education of young men and women.

Questions too are quite powerful ways to focus attention. Just like professors do in a classroom with students, when leaders ask questions they send people on mental journeys—quests—in search of answers. The questions that leaders ask send messages about what's most important to them and reinforce the focus of their department or program. Questions constitute one more measure of how serious you are about your espoused beliefs; the nature and substance of your questions reveal the values that should be attended to and how much energy should be devoted to them.

The importance of raising questions was a key leadership insight for Jackie Schmidt-Posner in her job in the public service center and as the institutional adviser for a large student-run conference. She purposefully asked questions that "brought the student coordinators back to the vision and purpose of the project. Once they had their eye on the ball, they could develop the necessary strategies." Jackie realized that a significant part of her role was often "to focus the group through asking the tough questions." Think about how your questions can frame the issue and set the agenda.[10]

Questions can help people escape the trap of their own paradigms by broadening their perspectives and enabling them to take responsibility for their own viewpoints. Asking questions can do the same for you. The process forces you to listen attentively to the people around you and what they are saying. This action demonstrates your respect for their ideas and opinions. If you are genuinely interested in what other people have to say, you need to ask their opinion, especially before giving your own. Asking what others think facilitates their participation in decision-making and often increases support for the resulting choice. Asking the right questions reduces the risk that a decision might be undermined by either inadequate consideration or unexpected opposition. Of course, you must not only listen to their responses but also be open to giving their feedback serious consideration in subsequent decisions. Sincerity must underlie the asking.

Develop Your Competence

Words alone do not make a leader credible. Having a clear and authentic message is a necessary first step, but the ability to consistently deliver the message and act on it requires a high level of skill. Before you can do the right things, you have to know *how* to do them. You cannot do what you don't know how to do, no matter how moral or noble the purpose and regardless of whether others affirm the direction.

To commit to doing something without the capacity to perform it is either disingenuous or stupid. There's nothing courageous about boldly saying you'll successfully launch a new curriculum or turn around a residential learning community if you have neither the skills nor the resources to do it. Leaders must be aware of the degree to which they have the capabilities to do what they say. And if they lack the competence, they must dedicate themselves to continuous learning and improvement.

This is something Jackie kept firmly in mind when working with the students on the conference. As she said, "I shared my own learnings with the students—including past mistakes—and I was willing to change direction based on new information." She made sure that she was part of the learning community and, rather than frame herself as an expert, she acknowledged areas (student culture and schedules, as just two examples) about which the students knew more and could teach her.

Acquiring competence involves being honest with yourself about your abilities. People who exaggerate their abilities to perform a task or achieve a goal, or who inflate their claims of possessing admirable qualities or desirable material goods, are called phonies and fakes and are seldom followed for very long. Your value as a leader is determined by your guiding beliefs and your ability to act on them.

To be genuine requires that you honestly and continuously assess your existing capabilities and are willing to learn new ones. Keep in mind that left untended, everyone's skills and abilities, like any other asset, deteriorate over time. And it should come as no surprise to anyone on a college campus that learning takes time and conscious attention. If leaders expect others to do things that they have never done before, which is the basis for any improvement or innovative effort, fostering a climate in which people can learn and be unafraid to admit what they don't know is essential. Such a climate occurs only in those situations in which leaders also Model the Way by participating in the learning process themselves.

QUESTIONS FOR REFLECTION: *MODEL THE WAY*

The first step you must take along the path to becoming an exemplary leader is inward. It's a step toward discovering and owning your personal values and beliefs. In finding your voice, you'll discern the principles that guide your decisions and actions and be able to express yourself in unique ways. And in affirming shared values, you'll strengthen commitment to principles that everyone should uphold.

Setting the example is the *doing* part of what you *say* you will do. Walking the talk is the first test of your credibility. Leaders are measured by the consistency of their deeds and words. You must show up, pay attention, and participate directly in the process of making extraordinary things happen. It's the consistency between words and actions that builds credibility, and you earn it moment by moment. Leading by example is how you make visions and values tangible. It's how you provide the *evidence* that you are believable, competent, and personally dedicated.

In developing your competence in the leadership practice of Model the Way, spend some time reflecting on the following questions. After you've given them sufficient consideration, let others know what you are thinking and willing to do.

▶ What are your three most important values? What are the most important values of your work team/organization? Where is the common ground between your values and theirs?

▶ How do your values influence and guide your leadership actions? How do your daily actions and calendar reflect, or not reflect, your espoused values? How can you make explicit the link between your values and the decisions you make? What can you do to reduce any gaps between your espoused values and your actions (or those of your team)?

▶ In this academic year, what are the differences (changes) you aspire to make? How can you ensure that these are connected with shared values?

▶ What do you hope people will say about you when your term is completed? What do you need to be doing right now for this to be true in the future?

CHAPTER 3

Inspire a Shared Vision

JOAN CARTER TOOK OVER as general manager and executive chef of the university's Adobe Lodge when both membership and sales had been severely declining for several years. Faculty and staff were unhappy, the restaurant's balance sheet was "scary," and her team was divided into factions.

Joan took all of this in, but what she saw was a dusty diamond. "I saw a beautiful and historic building full of mission-era flavor and character that should be, could be, and would be *the* place on campus." In her mind's eye, she saw the Lodge bustling. She saw professors and university staff chatting on the lovely enclosed patio and enjoying high-quality, appealing, yet inexpensive meals. She smiled as she envisioned her team assisting alumni in planning beautiful, personal, and professionally catered wedding receptions and anniversary celebrations.

Joan could see a happy staff whose primary concern was customer satisfaction, a kitchen that produced a product far superior to "banquet food," and a catering staff who did whatever it took to make an event exceptional. She wasn't quite sure how the Lodge had deteriorated to the extent it had, but that really didn't matter. She decided to ignore the quick fix and set out to teach everyone how unique and magnificent the restaurant could be.

Over the next two years as she talked with customers and worked with her staff, she instilled a vision of the Lodge as a restaurant that celebrated good food and good company. As food and service quality began to improve, smiles became more prevalent among customers and staff, and sales started to rise: 20 percent the first year and 30 percent the next. When a senior university business manager asked Joan how she had turned the finances around so quickly and dramatically, she responded, "You can't turn around numbers. The balance sheet is just a reflection of what's happening here every day in the restaurant. I just helped the staff realize what we're really all about. It was always here," she said, "only perhaps a little dusty, a little ignored, and a little unloved. I just helped them see it."

The leaders we interviewed shared with Joan the perspective that bringing meaning to life in the present by focusing on improving life in the future is essential to making extraordinary things happen. All enterprises and projects, big and small, originate in the mind's eye; they begin with imagination and the belief that what's now only an image can one day be made real.

To be an exemplary leader, you must be able to imagine a positive future. When you envision the future you want for yourself and others, and when you feel passionate about the legacy you want to leave, you are much more likely to take that first step. But if you don't have the slightest clue about your hopes, dreams, and aspirations, the chance that you'll take the lead is nil. In fact, you may not even see the opportunity that's right there in front of you.

But it's not just about *your* vision. It's about having a *shared* vision. Everyone has dreams, aspirations, and the desire that tomorrow be better than today. When visions are shared, they attract more people, sustain higher levels of motivation, and withstand more challenges than those that are singular. You must ensure that what you can see is also something that others can see and vice versa.

The most effective leaders in higher education are those who most frequently Inspire a Shared Vision. We asked direct reports how often their leaders engaged in the six behaviors associated with Inspire a Shared Vision on the *Leadership Practices Inventory,* with assessments ranging from 1 (Almost never) to 10 (Almost always). We also asked them a separate question about the extent to which they agreed or disagreed with the statement *Overall, this person is an effective leader* (1 = Strongly disagree and 5 = Strongly agree). The analysis showed that the effectiveness ratings of leaders by their direct reports increased systematically ($p < 0.001$) as leaders were observed engaging more and more frequently in the behaviors associated with inspiring a shared vision. There was a remarkable 85 percent bump in effectiveness from the bottom to the top quartile.

CLARIFY YOUR VISION

No matter what term is used—*vision, purpose, mission, legacy, dream, calling,* or *burning agenda*—the intent is the same. People who exercise leadership want to do something significant and accomplish something that no one else has yet achieved. What that something is—that sense of meaning and purpose—must come from within. That's why, just as we said about values, you must first clarify your own visions of the future before you can expect to enlist others in a shared vision. To create a climate of meaningfulness, first you must believe in something yourself. Before you can inspire others, *you* must be inspired. Your passion is an indicator of what you feel most deeply about and find worthwhile in and of itself. It's a clue to what is *intrinsically* rewarding to you.

You can't impose a vision on others. It must be something that has meaning to them, not just to you. Leaders must foster conditions under which people will do things because they *want* to, not because they have to. One of *the* most important practices of leadership is giving life and work a sense of meaning and purpose by offering an exciting vision of the future that could be better than what exists at the moment.[1] Leaders structure environments so that personal values and department, program, or institutional visions intersect. For example, people's answer to the question about how often their leader "shows others how their long-term interests can be realized by enlisting in a common vision" was strongly related to the extent to which they felt they were making a difference in their organization, as shown in figure 3.1.

In this digital age, people often ask, "How can I have a vision of what's going to happen on this campus, or in this state, let alone in the grander business of higher education, five or 10 or even two years from now, when I don't even know what's going to happen next week

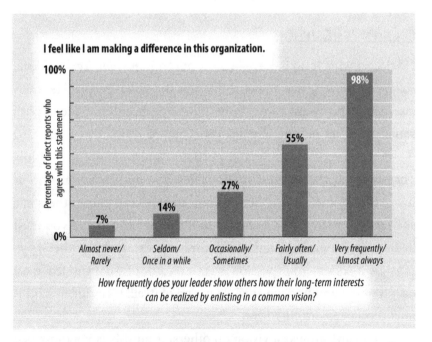

Figure 3.1 People feel they are making a difference in their organizations in direct relationship to the frequency they report that their leader shows others how their long-term interests can be realized by enlisting in a common vision.

or even over this next term?" Here are a couple of ways of answering this question. First, Martin Luther King Jr. spoke poignantly about his dream, but he also said that you don't have to see the whole staircase to take the first step. So long as you have some idea about where you are going, you can take the next step.

Another way to think about this is to imagine you're driving along the Pacific Coast Highway heading south from San Francisco on a bright, sunny day. The hills are on your left, the ocean on your right. On some curves the cliffs plunge several hundred feet to the water. You can see for miles and miles. You're cruising along at the speed limit, tunes blaring, top down, wind in your hair, and not a care in the world. Suddenly, without warning, you come around a bend in the road, and there's a blanket of fog as thick as you've ever seen it. *What do you do?* We've asked this question many, many times, and we get the same answers: "I slow way down, turn my lights on, grab the steering wheel with both hands, tense up, lean forward, and turn off the radio." Then you go around the next curve in the road, the fog has lifted, and it's clear again. What do you do? Relax, turn the lights off, speed up, turn the radio back on, and enjoy the scenery.

This analogy illustrates the importance of clarity of vision, *especially* what it takes to move ahead quickly and confidently. How fast can you drive in the fog without risking your own or other people's lives? How comfortable are you riding in a car with someone who drives fast in the fog? Are you able to drive more quickly when it's foggy or when it's clear? It's obvious, isn't it? You can go more quickly when your vision is clear.

Discover Your Theme

Just knowing that having a vision is essential doesn't make one manifest over your head like a light bulb. When we ask people to tell us where their visions come from, they often have great difficulty describing the process. And when they do provide an answer, typically it's more about a feeling, a sense, a hunch, a gut reaction. After all, there's no map or interstate highway to the future. When people first take on their roles as leaders—whether they're appointed or they step forward and volunteer—they often don't have a *clear* vision of the future.

In the beginning what leaders on college campuses typically have is a *theme*. They have concerns, desires, hypotheses, propositions, arguments, hopes, and dreams—core concepts around which they organize their aspirations and actions. Leaders often begin the process of envisioning the future by discovering their themes. What leaders eventually say about their vision is an elaboration, an interpretation, and a variation on those themes. Fortunately, there are ways to improve your ability to articulate your themes, and ultimately your visions, of the future.[2]

For example, finding your vision, like finding your voice, is a process of self-exploration and self-creation. It's an intuitive, emotional undertaking. There's often no logic to it. What we've seen is that exemplary leaders have a passion for their departments, their causes, their programs, their students, their subject matter, their technologies, their communities—something other than their own fame and fortune. Leaders care about something much bigger than themselves and much bigger than all of us. Leaders care about making a difference by changing the status quo in some meaningful way.

And emotions are contagious. If you don't care deeply about something, how can you expect others to feel any sense of conviction? How can you expect others to get jazzed if you're not energized and excited yourself? How can you expect others to suffer through the inevitable long hours and hard work if you're not similarly committed?

We asked Kent Koth why he selected a particular project as his Personal-Best Leadership Experience. His answer speaks volumes about how in leading others we discover our own passions: "This was the defining moment in my budding professional life. It was at this moment that I knew what I was born to do. I had found my place in the world."

Kent wanted to provide an educational and service opportunity for students to engage with issues and people with whom they were unfamiliar. As a community outreach program coordinator, he traveled to San Francisco with a group of students for the campus's first-ever "alternative" spring break. This group slept on the floor of a downtown church and worked at local homeless shelters. Each night they cooked dinner together and discussed the day's events as they ate. After dinner they gathered as a group to participate in team-building exercises, talk about social issues related to their service experiences, write in the group's journal, and prepare for the next day's work.

His fondest wish for the project, Kent told us, "was for students to return to campus with a new sense of passion and commitment to social justice. I hoped the trip would serve as the spark to ignite a lifelong exploration of commitment to others. I dreamed that these students would come away stronger, wiser, and more compassionate." Kent discovered his theme: "I possessed a passion for justice that motivated me to construct a project that would raise complicated ethical issues. Everyone is equal. Everyone has a gift to give. Everyone has something to learn. Love and justice can guide us to a new level of awareness."

Explore Your Past

As contradictory as it might seem, in aiming for the future you need to look back to your past. Looking backward can actually enable you to see farther than if you only stare straight ahead. Understanding your personal history can help you identify themes, patterns, and beliefs that both underscore why you care about particular issues or circumstances now and explain why making them better in the future is such a high priority.

Consider the journey taken by William Hwang, who founded United InnoWorks Academy, a nonprofit dedicated to opening the world of science and engineering to middle-school students from disadvantaged backgrounds; it aims to not only ignite their love of learning but also inspire volunteerism in college students. His passion was sparked when he reflected on his own experiences in high school, when he had attended several special summer programs that were "born from someone's imagination and hard work...that changed, reshaped, and influenced me in amazing ways. They helped me focus, opened my eyes to new and exciting possibilities."

William remembered a track teammate who had few role models and was on probation throughout high school; thinking about him sparked, as William explained, "a burning desire to do something to help others who might be lacking the same opportunities." He decided to devote himself to something that could bring opportunities of the kind he had to underprivileged children who needed them the most, and the United InnoWorks Academy was born. Beginning with a single program in 2003, InnoWorks has nurtured more than 2,400 students at 14 university chapters around the world, and those numbers continue to grow.

As William learned to appreciate, when you gaze first into your past, you elongate your future. You also magnify your future and give it detail as, like William, you recall the richness of your past experiences. So, to envision the possibilities in the distant future, look first to the past. When you do, you're likely to find that your central theme has been there for a long time.

In addition to identifying lifelong themes, there's another benefit to looking back before looking ahead: you can gain a greater appreciation for how long it can take to fulfill aspirations. You also realize that many, many paths can be pursued and that there may be new summits that you want to climb.

None of this is to say that the past *is* your future. Adopting that extremely dangerous perspective would be like trying to drive to the future while looking only in the rearview mirror. From that angle you'd drive yourself and your program right off a cliff. The point is to avail yourself of the widest variety of experiences possible. Broaden your experiences and expand your network of connections. As you do that, your time horizons will also stretch forward.

Immerse Yourself

As you gain experience, you naturally acquire information about what happens, how things happen, and who makes things happen in an organization, in a profession, on a campus, or within an industry. When you're presented with an unfamiliar problem, you consciously (or unconsciously) draw on your experiences to help solve it. You select crucial information, make relevant comparisons, and integrate lessons you've learned with the current situation. For the experienced leader, all of this may happen in a matter of seconds. But it's the years of direct contact with a variety of problems and situations that equip the leader with unique insight; listening, reading, feeling, and sensing—these experiences improve the leader's vision. Leaders develop an intuitive sense of what is going to happen down the road—they can anticipate what is just around the corner. They are also sufficiently self-aware to recognize their biases because having experience and expertise can also blind you to new, important information. Exemplary leaders take care to look beyond the data that confirms their initial judgments.[3]

Remember, if you don't believe that something can change for the better, you are unlikely to take any action; as a result, you will be right—few things improve all by themselves. To exercise leadership, you must believe yourself before anyone else will believe that they should come aboard with you. Jo-Anne Shibles spoke of this feeling as a "gut reaction" that, in her case, told her that the Student Leadership Institute she was asked to develop was not just something that could be established but that it would make a significant difference for students and others on campus. Jo-Anne, the activities coordinator within the office of student life, believed right from the start that she could quickly and successfully get the institute up and running.

The prospect excited her, and she could visualize in some detail how the program would operate and who might be involved in it. As she told us: "I could see students sitting in a class, listening to a faculty member talk with them about ethical dilemmas and slippery slopes. I could see small groups of students talking about how different cultural backgrounds influence our leadership behaviors. I could see students taking on more active roles in their organizations. I could see how excited students would be to get their certificates at our reception at the end of the program." From her initial gut feeling—and lots of hard work—came a successful pilot program in which 50 students explored their leadership styles and developed leadership skills. Now, many years later, the project still makes Jo-Anne smile—and it continues on the campus, inspiring an ever-growing group of student leaders.

Like Jo-Anne, many of the people we interviewed mentioned that the exercise of analyzing their Personal-Best Leadership Experiences was enlightening for them: by highlighting critical lessons from the past, they were able to generate insightful road maps for leadership highways still to be explored. The knowledge gained from direct experience and active searching, once stored in the subconscious, becomes the basis for leaders' intuition, insight, and vision.

Envisioning the future is a process that begins with an inspiration, a feeling, or a sense that something is worth doing. Your vision of the future may be fuzzy, but at least you're focused on a meaningful theme. You believe that the present situation could be better than it is today. You act on your instincts, and the vision gets a little clearer. You do something else that moves you forward, and the vision gets clearer still. You pay attention to it, experience it, immerse yourself in it. You get the ball rolling, and over time you see more detail in your dream.

It's an iterative process, one that eventually results in something that you and others can articulate.

GET OTHERS ON BOARD

Visions are about hopes, dreams, and aspirations. They're declarations of a strong desire to achieve something ambitious. They're expressions of optimism. Can you imagine a leader enlisting others in a cause by saying, "I'd like you to join me in doing the ordinary"? Not likely. Visions stretch people to imagine exciting possibilities, breakthrough programs, and revolutionary social change. Grand aspirations such as these cannot be achieved, however, until they are shared by your constituents—the staff, faculty, administration, students, alumni, donors, or others you want to enlist. This is exactly what Derek McCormack, vice chancellor, told us about the time he was charged with growing the institution. He realized that his job "wasn't to find a vision myself but to create a shared vision so that we could all go on the same journey together."

It's not enough for a leader to have a vision; the members of the leader's department must also understand, accept, and commit to it. When others shared with us their Personal-Best Leadership Experiences, they made comments similar to Derek's. People frequently talked about the need to get buy-in from others on the vision. They explained how they had to communicate the purpose and build support for a unified direction. They knew that everyone had to commit to a common purpose. They understood that to get everyone on the same journey, they had to be able to communicate *why* others should want to join in, what it would mean to them, and how it would benefit them. While *you* might be able to see how others' interests are served, if they can't see how their needs are connected to the larger vision, they will be reluctant to climb aboard. But when they do, the department's and the institution's ability to change and reach its potential soars.

Getting others on board means you need to listen deeply. From the conversations you have with constituents, you need to find a common purpose that unites potentially diverse motivations and aspirations. You need to be able to instill a sense of pride in being unique. You need to paint pictures that make the vision come alive, and you need to speak with conviction and enthusiasm about the exciting possibilities.

Listen Deeply

Identifying who your constituents are and discovering their common aspirations are required steps that leaders must take in enlisting others. No matter how grand the dream of an individual visionary, if others don't see in it the possibility of realizing their own hopes and desires, they won't follow. You must show others how they too will be served by the long-term vision of the future and how their specific needs can be satisfied.

What this takes is attentive listening so that you can sense the purpose in others. By knowing your constituents, listening to them, and soliciting their advice, you are better able to give voice to their concerns. You can stand before others and say with assurance, "Here's what I heard you say that you want for yourselves. Here's how your own needs and interests will be served by enlisting in a common cause." In a sense, leaders hold up a mirror and reflect back to their constituents what they say they most desire. When people see that reflection, they recognize themselves and can embrace the image.

Appreciating that leadership is a relationship puts listening in its proper perspective. It has been said that no great idea enters the mind through an open mouth. Exemplary leaders know that they need not have all the ideas or all the answers themselves. The origin of a vision does not arise from gazing at a crystal ball; there are clues all around you if you are able to listen for them as they are passed on from students, colleagues, alumni, parents, and donors. There is no shortage of ideas and opportunities for making your part of the institution even better than it already is.

To accurately and faithfully hear what constituents want—what they hope to make you understand, appreciate, and include in the vision—requires periodically suspending regular activities and spending time simply listening to others. Get to know your constituents by visiting their hangouts; go to sporting events, recitals, dining halls, the library, lectures, and classes. Get out of your office and wander into the offices of faculty and staff colleagues. Have coffee, breakfast, lunch, afternoon breaks, or some unstructured time with constituent groups. Find out what's going on with them and what they are hoping to achieve from their relationship with you and your program.

Discover a Common Purpose

Have you asked people in your department or program why they stay? More likely, and especially if staffing is part of your responsibilities, you worry about turnover, retention rates, and why people leave. Instead think about the vast majority of those who stay and ask *them* why they stick around. Why do you? The most important reason people give about why they don't leave or aren't looking for another position is that they find the work they are doing to be challenging, meaningful, and purposeful.

Academic institutions, on both the faculty and staff sides, have an advantage over many other types of organizations in that our colleagues generally start out with a shared commitment to learning and personal and professional development. Listening with sensitivity to the aspirations of others reveals common values that link everyone on campus. People want a chance to be tested, a chance to make it on their own, to take part in a social experiment, to do something well, to do something good, and to change the way things are.[4] Aren't these the essence of what most leadership opportunities are all about?

What people want from their workplace has not changed very dramatically over the years despite economic upturns and downturns. Regardless of profession, industry, or location, people rank "interesting work" well above "high income" as important. And the quality of leadership ("working for a leader with vision and values") is even more motivating than dollars. Would it surprise you that the most frequently mentioned measure of success in work life is "personal satisfaction for doing a good job"? People cite this between three and four times as often as "getting ahead" or "making a good living."[5]

Universities have seldom been places where people go to work to maximize their financial gains. There's considerable opportunity for campus leaders to appeal to much more than material rewards. Great leaders evoke meaning. The values and interests of freedom, self-actualization, learning, community, excellence, justice, service, and social responsibility truly attract people to a common cause. Shared visions are "a force in people's hearts, a force of impressive power."[6]

There is a deep human yearning to make a difference. People want to know that they're doing something meaningful on this earth, that there's a purpose to their existence. Work can provide that purpose, and increasingly the workplace is where people pursue meaning and identity.[7] The best university-based leaders are able to bring out and make use of this human longing by communicating the meaning and significance of the college's work so that people understand their own important role in perpetuating it. When leaders clearly communicate a shared vision of an organization, they ennoble those who work on its behalf. They elevate the human spirit.

Take Pride in Being Unique

Visions communicate what makes the team, department, school, or university singular and unequaled; they set the organization apart from all others. There is no advantage to working for an institution that does precisely the same thing as the one across town. For students, faculty, staff, or alumni to want to sign up with you, they first must understand how what you are proposing is distinctive and stands out from the crowd. Uniqueness fosters pride. It boosts the self-respect and self-esteem of everyone associated with the organization. The prouder people are of the college where they work, their students and graduates, the more engaged they are likely to be.

For example, when describing one of her most admired leaders, Lina Chen told us, "She made me feel proud; she made me feel that what I was doing was special and made a unique contribution." Lina worked in the university's research lab with renowned scientists, but she was neither a scholar nor a researcher. She was responsible for computer support and making sure that all the equipment was up and running without any issues. However, she says, this wasn't how her leader described what her job responsibilities were:

> She began by explaining to me the importance of the research that was being done and how it could impact the lives of many people. Furthermore, the more accurate our results from the research were, the more beneficial it will be to those who are involved because we can help improve their quality of life. To keep the computer equipment up and running is crucial because it makes the researchers' jobs easier. You are helping them in improving the environment and making the world a better place.

For Lina this "made my job very meaningful and inspiring to be part of a team that is making a difference in the world."

Leaders like Lina's get people excited about signing on for their vision by making sure that everyone involved feels that what they do is unique and believes that they play a crucial role regardless of job title or specific responsibilities. Feeling unique also enables smaller units within larger institutions to have their own vision while still being part of the collective one. Although every unit (department, program, or school) within a university must be aligned with the overall organizational vision, it can express its unique purpose within the larger whole. Every function and every department can differentiate itself by finding its most distinctive qualities. Each can be proud of the ideal and unique image of its future as it works toward the collective future of the larger institution.

Invoke Images of the Future

A beacon of light cutting through the fog is an image you can picture in your mind. Leaders often talk about the future with such visual references. They speak about foresight, focus, forecasts, future scenarios, points of view, and new perspectives. Visions are images in the mind, and leaders make them real to others by making them more concrete and tangible. They bring impressions to life by painting word pictures. As shown in figure 3.2, the more frequently that leaders were seen as "describing a compelling image of what our future could look like,"

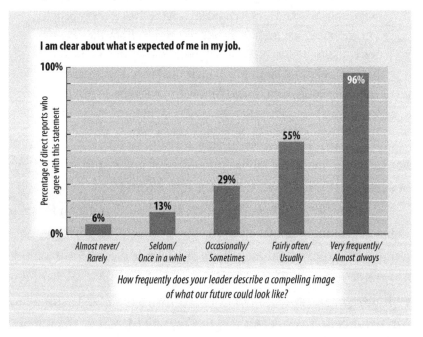

Figure 3.2 People's clarity about what is expected of them in their jobs increases with the frequency to which leaders describe a compelling image of what our future could look like.

the more their direct reports indicated that they were clear about what was expected of them in their jobs.

In our workshops and classes, we often use an exercise to illustrate the power of painting word pictures. We ask people to think about the city of Paris, France, and to shout out the first thing that comes to mind. The replies—the Eiffel Tower, the Arc de Triomphe, the Seine, Notre Dame, good food, wine, romance—all are images of real places and real sensations. No one calls out the kilometers, population, or gross domestic product of Paris. The same would be true for your college or university campus. Why? Human memory is stored in images and sensory impressions, not in numbers. We recall images of reality, not abstractions from it.

When you invent the future, you need to get a mental picture of what things will be like long before you begin the journey. Images are your windows on the world of tomorrow. When talking about taking people (your department or program) to places they have never been before, you start by imagining what this would look like. For example, in spreading the word across campus about the new Student Leadership Institute, Jo-Anne helped others imagine it. She emphasized "that the program had not been done before." She told students being recruited for the pilot project: "This is new. It is going to be great—and you are part of making it great. Imagine being able to learn how to build a team within your club, deal with someone who is sloughing off on their job, or run an effective meeting." Jo-Anne conveyed vivid images of the concrete skills that students would gain by being involved. She explained how they could do all of this in a few hours a week, in time between classes. By spending time one-on-one and in small groups, she made the vision real and enlisted others in it.

Just as Jo-Anne did, leaders animate the vision and make manifest the purpose so that others can see it, hear it, taste it, touch it, feel it. Leaders make full use of the power of language in communicating a shared identity and giving life to visions. Successful leaders use metaphors and other figures of speech to lend vividness and tangibility to abstract ideas. Leaders draw word pictures, give examples, tell stories, and relate anecdotes. They find ways of giving expression to their hopes for the future. In making the intangible vision tangible, leaders ignite constituents' passion and develop a shared sense of destiny.

Lori Ann Roth, her university's director of training and organizational development, told us about another method for conveying a shared image of the future—one that involved not just word pictures but actual pictures. She described how her team developed a literal vision board: They attached their mission statement to foam core poster board, and everyone added pictures, words, feelings, or phrases that resonated with this, then they mounted it all on a wall in a common area. "When you looked at it, you could actually feel the team spirit and emotion that went into creating the vision," Lori said. "Seeing the vision board every day reminded each of us to do something to move forward toward our vision."

Leaders like Lori and Jo-Anne teach others the vision. They engage constituents in conversations about their lives, their own hopes and dreams, and how they can see these realized by sharing and participating in the vision. Lori, Jo-Anne, and other exemplary leaders know they can't impose their personal dream on others. They know that creating a common vision is about developing a *shared* sense of destiny. It's about enrolling others so that they can *see* how their own interests and aspirations are aligned with the vision and can thereby become mobilized to commit their individual energies to its realization.

Similarly, Sean Collins knew he had to engage with others on campus to conjure a unified picture of what could be. When he became director of environment, health, and safety, the campus research and teaching laboratories were not uniformly safe from chemical spills, and there were unlabeled containers everywhere. His vision was to establish and maintain spaces that were 100 percent safe and in so doing to cultivate a culture of safety on campus.

He was confident that the faculty implicitly shared this vision because "no faculty member would want their students to get hurt or their laboratories shut down by inspection agencies." He knew that he couldn't make decisions unilaterally, and, moreover, he couldn't personally be on hand in every lab at all hours of the day to ensure that safety standards were being met. This meant that he had to get others to embrace his vision and *want* to make their labs as safe as possible for everyone involved. He spent lots of time listening to the people directly responsible for the labs, highlighting their areas of shared concerns and aspirations and collaborating to find solutions that worked for everyone involved. In the end he was able to go from something that was implicitly shared to something that faculty explicitly supported.

Practice Positive Communication and Be Expressive

To foster team spirit, breed optimism, promote resilience, and renew faith and confidence, leaders learn to look on the bright side. They keep hope alive. They strengthen their constituents' belief that struggles today will produce a more promising tomorrow.

People want leaders with enthusiasm, with a bounce in their step and a positive attitude, because this conveys that they'll be participating in an invigorating journey. People with a can-do attitude are followed, not those cynics who give 10 reasons why something can't be done or who don't make others feel good about themselves or what they're doing. Naysayers only stop forward progress; they do not start it.

Researchers working with neural networks have documented that when people feel rebuffed or left out, the brain activates a site for registering physical pain.[8] People actually remember downbeat comments far more often, in greater detail, and with more intensity than they do encouraging words. When negative remarks become a preoccupation, people's brains lose mental efficiency. This is all the more reason for leaders to be positive. A positive approach to life broadens people's concepts of future possibilities, and these exciting options build on one another.[9] In an affirming environment, people become more innovative and see more options. Those who enjoy more positivity are also better able to cope with adversities and are more resilient during times of high stress, which is a vital capacity when dealing with uncertain and challenging times.

The leaders people admire most are energetic, vigorous, active, and full of life. Randi DuBois, one of the founders of Pro-Action, gets people to stretch themselves by engaging in challenging physical tasks. Typically, her clients are nervous, even a bit scared at first. But people of all ages, sizes, and physical abilities have successfully completed her outdoor challenge courses. How does Randi succeed in leading these people? Her secret is very simple: she's always positive that people can do the course, and she never says *never*. We have watched her in programs with our students and colleagues as she conveys very clearly that people have the power within themselves to accomplish whatever they desire. (Both authors know this from personal experience, as we have been 40 feet above the ground, leaping off a small platform for an iron ring while Randi cheered us on.)

In discussions on why particular leaders have a magnetic effect, they are often described as charismatic. But *charisma* has become such an overused and misused term that it's almost useless as a descriptor of leaders. For instance, leadership scholars note that "in the popular media, *charisma* has come to mean anything ranging from chutzpah to Pied Piperism, from celebrity to superman status. It has become an overworked cliché for strong, attractive, and inspiring personality."[10]

To better understand this elusive quality, social scientists have observed the behavior of individuals who are deemed charismatic. What they've found is that such people are just more animated than others. They smile more, speak faster, pronounce words more clearly, and move their heads and bodies more often. They are also more likely to reach out and touch or make some physical contact with others during greetings.[11] Accordingly, *charisma* can be better understood as *expressiveness.*

People often underestimate their abilities to be expressive. We've found that people's common perception of themselves as uninspiring is in sharp contrast to their performance when talking about their Personal-Best Leadership Experiences or their ideal futures—or even their upcoming holidays and vacations. When relating hopes, dreams, and successes, people are almost always emotionally expressive. Expressiveness comes naturally when talking about deep desires for the future: People lean forward in their chairs and move their arms about, their eyes light up, their voices sing with emotion, and they smile. They are enthusiastic, articulate, optimistic, and uplifting. Emotions drive expressiveness.[12] In short, people *are* inspiring! What's required is being willing to share your enthusiasm with others, rather than locking it away and assuming that expressiveness is somehow "not professional." Leaders who make a difference on campus have a passion for what they are doing and lead from the heart.

QUESTIONS FOR REFLECTION: *INSPIRE A SHARED VISION*

Visions give focus to human energy. This enables each person connected with the department, program, or institution to see more clearly what's ahead of them and what the future will look like when everyone has added their piece. With this in mind, they can contribute to the whole, efficiently and with confidence.

But visions seen only by the leaders are insufficient to generate organized movement. You must get others to see the exciting possibilities. You breathe life into visions by communicating the hopes and dreams of others so that they clearly understand how their values and interests will be served by a particular long-term vision of the future. Speak about your own convictions and the uniqueness of your organization, and make others proud to be part of something special. Be upbeat and expressive and attract followers with your energy, optimism, and hopeful outlook.

In developing your competence in the leadership practice of Inspire a Shared Vision, spend some time reflecting on the following questions. After you've given them sufficient consideration, let others know what you are thinking and willing to do.

▶ How have your past experiences shaped the important themes in your life and what you bring to the workplace? Why do you care about the work you and your team are doing? What were you doing or discussing the last time you became animated about your work?

▶ How can you describe the difference you hope to make and why it would benefit others (students, faculty, staff, or alumni)? What hope, wish, or dream do you have for yourself as a leader and for the contributions of your team or department to your institution?

▶ How can you find out from your team members how they explain to their friends and colleagues not just what they do but why what they do matters? What do they brag about to people outside your department or institution? What patterns do you hear in their responses, and can you use this as a mantra for inspiring your department?

▶ When recruiting someone to join your team, how can you illustrate what you do—and why you do it—that makes the work of your unit significant and meaningful?

Challenge the Process

WHEN KIM LOEB BECAME EXECUTIVE DIRECTOR of Professional, Applied and Continuing Education (PACE), the program was small and losing money. She immediately set about restructuring PACE by overhauling programs and courses that hadn't been updated in decades, refocusing initiatives on student services and bringing in professional development resources to ensure that her team was working to full capacity. Within five years Kim's program offered more than 600 full- and part-time programs, courses, and workshops. It recruited students from more than 30 different countries and generated over $1 million in revenue. "People say it's so great your university sends you on international recruitment trips," Kim told us. "But no; they don't send me. We create these opportunities."

Much of the credit for PACE's new directions is due to Kim's encouraging her team to consider innovative ideas and opportunities. She does not feel threatened by ideas or skill sets that differ from her own. Instead she sees each of her team members as having something unique to offer: "I always try to bring in people for our team who have different skills than me." Her openness and vulnerability helped her expand PACE in directions that wouldn't be possible if working on her own.

Of course the accomplishments at PACE don't mean that every change has been a success. "We've definitely developed some programs that weren't winners," Kim told us. She knows that being successful means you have to be willing to fail, and she fosters that same understanding within her team. It's okay to make mistakes, Kim said, so long as your team can learn from them. One way she shows her team and university that she's open to feedback and growth is by attending lunch with class participants and writing up a report based on the improvements and constructive criticism she hears from them.

Getting people to venture beyond the limitations they usually set for themselves and experiencing victory over doubt are keys to their effectiveness. This triumph is significant because the challenges facing colleges and universities demand a willingness to take risks and experiment with innovation. Leaders foster risk-taking and encourage others to step into the unknown rather than play it safe. They set goals that are higher than current levels but not so steep that people feel only frustration. Leaders raise the bar gradually and offer coaching and training to build skills that help people get up and through each new level.

In our interviews and case studies, we asked people to tell us about their Personal-Best Leadership Experiences. Invariably, they talked about times of change, difficulty, and adversity. We didn't ask them about times of change. We asked them about their personal bests, but they chose to write about times of change. This response underscores the fact that leadership is inherently associated with change and challenge. It involves doing things differently, experimenting, and taking risks. Leadership without change is entirely ceremonial. You can't lead yourself, your department, or your institution to a better tomorrow without change. Doing your best as a leader means that you must Challenge the Process.

We asked direct reports how often their leaders engaged in the six behaviors associated with Challenge the Process on the *Leadership*

Practices Inventory, with assessments ranging from 1 (Almost never) to 10 (Almost always). We also asked them a separate question about the extent to which they agreed or disagreed with the statement *Overall, this person is an effective leader* (1 = Strongly disagree and 5 = Strongly agree). How effective direct reports rate their leaders increases systematically ($p < 0.001$) as leaders are observed engaging more and more frequently in the behaviors associated with challenging the process. There was a huge 84 percent bump in effectiveness from the bottom to the top quartile.

SEIZE THE INITIATIVE TO IMPROVE

Colleges and universities are not typically bastions of change, often quite the contrary. Faculty often cling to what's familiar, administrations can be slow to adopt new systems and processes, and alumni love the traditions. Still, within the hallowed halls change is central to every institution's DNA. After all, students will be changed by the institutional experience. Otherwise, what's the point? As Jeffrey Buller, author of numerous books on higher education, has acknowledged, "In an academic setting, we need to set ourselves a loftier goal than simply settling for the status quo."[1]

Challenge the Process is not about change just for the sake of change but, consistent with higher education's purpose, change for the better. Leaders on college campuses are motivated by making the status quo not merely different but better. Improving the current situation demands change. It would be foolish to expect better results just by doing the same things over and over again.

Within and outside higher education, when people tell the stories of their Personal-Best Leadership Experiences they talk about the challenge of change. When we look at leaders, we see that their work is associated with adversity, uncertainty, hardship, disruption, transformation, transition, recovery, and new beginnings. Sometimes the changes are small and sometimes they are large, but they are all about awakening new possibilities. Leaders don't always have to change history, but they do have to make a change in "business as usual."

When asked about who initiated the projects that they selected as their Personal-Best Leadership Experiences, we assumed that most people would name themselves. Instead more than half the cases were initiated by someone other than the leader—usually the person's immediate supervisor, manager, department chair, director, or dean. Yet if leadership is about seizing the initiative, how can people be called "leaders" when they are assigned the jobs and tasks they undertake?

As we see it, the fact that more than half the cases were not self-initiated is quite positive. It liberates the people who thought they had to kickstart all the changes themselves, and it encourages the idea that responsibility for innovation and improvement is everyone's business. If the only times people reported doing their best were when they got to be the supervisor, department chair, director, or some head honcho, the majority of leadership experiences would evaporate—as would the majority of change both on and off campus. The reality is that much of what people do at work is assigned; few of us get to start anything from scratch. Leaders who were seen as "taking the initiative in anticipating and responding to change" were concomitantly assessed by their direct reports as bringing out the best of people's talents and abilities, as the analysis in figure 4.1 reveals.

Seizing the initiative has less to do with position than it does with attitude and action. Innovation and excellence are the results of people, at all levels, making things happen. It's no surprise, then, that when it comes to change and continuous improvement, everyone needs to believe that they can take the initiative to do something different. It's the responsibility of leaders to foster an environment in which that belief can become a reality.

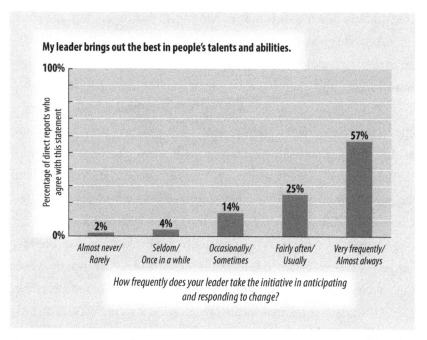

Figure 4.1 The more often leaders are seen as taking initiative in anticipating and responding to change the more they are viewed as bringing out the best in people's talents and abilities.

Encourage Initiative in Others

Innovative leaders seize the initiative, and they also encourage innovation and resourcefulness in others. You want people to speak up, to offer suggestions for improvement, and to be straightforward with their constructive criticism. Yet when it comes to situations that involve high uncertainty, high risk, and high challenge, many people feel reluctant to act, afraid they might make matters worse.

Because of its high visibility, the annual "You Can Make a Difference" conference had been heavily micromanaged by various staff members—that is, until Jackie Schmidt-Posner became the adviser to the students running the conference. As she said, "I challenged our staff to walk our talk and support student development by empowering our students to carry out the project. We had to step back and let the students learn from their experiences, even if they made some mistakes. This was risky because some of my colleagues felt the conference would not be of high quality if the students weren't closely monitored—and there was a chance they could have been right."

While Jackie admitted to being "a little nervous" at the start, she challenged the student leaders to excel by "constantly posing questions, asking them what their vision and goals were and how they could include and empower others to get there." She also encouraged and supported the students when they stumbled "to always learn from their experience." The conference turned out to be a huge success, engaging large numbers of students from very diverse backgrounds. A broader range of students assumed leadership roles in the conference than ever before. Not only did the program receive a university-based award but the two student coordinators also received individual service awards for their leadership.

Leaders like Jackie, who speak out and Challenge the Process, believe in their ability to do something about the situation they face. They also believe in their ability to help others.[2] People who are high in self-efficacy—the personal belief in how well one can handle prospective situations, capable of taking action to achieve a goal—are more likely to act than those who are not.

The most important way leaders instill this can-do attitude is by providing opportunities for people to gain mastery of a task, often one step at a time. Training is crucial to building self-efficacy and to encouraging initiative. Isn't it interesting, perhaps ironic, that "training"—the sine qua non of higher education—is too infrequently applied to the development of faculty and staff capabilities? Exemplary college and university leaders design and build learning opportunities for more than just the students. They fully appreciate that knowledge, like any institutional asset, deteriorates over time. They realize that people can't do what they don't know how to do. Short of firing everyone who doesn't come with all the skills intact—a virtual impossibility—capabilities need to be continuously upgraded. More and more higher-education institutions are recognizing the importance of lifelong learning by investing in administrative and management development programs (as opposed to content-based training) for faculty and staff alike.[3]

Leaders provide opportunities for people to exceed their previous levels of performance. They regularly set the bar higher. And the best leaders understand the importance of setting the bar at a level at which people feel they can succeed. Raise it too high, and people will fail; if they fail too often, they'll quit trying. Raise the bar a bit at a time, and eventually more people master the situation. This awareness of the human need for challenge and a sensitivity to the need to succeed is among the critical balancing skills of any leader.

Make Challenge Meaningful

When we've asked people to think of historical leaders whom, if alive today, they would *willingly* follow, all of those nominated were people with strong beliefs about matters of principle: Susan B. Anthony, Mustafa Kemal Ataturk, Jesus Christ, Winston Churchill, Mahatma Ghandi, Maria Klawe, Martin Luther King Jr., Wendy Kopp, Abraham Lincoln, Nelson Mandela, Golda Meir, and Eleanor Roosevelt, to name a few. Another consistent thread that's woven through the list of admired historical leaders is that they were all individuals who served during times of turbulence, conflict, innovation, and change. They're people who triumphed against tremendous odds, who took initiative when there was inertia, who confronted tradition and the established order, and who mobilized people and institutions in the face of stiff resistance.

Leadership and challenge are inextricably linked, just as leadership and principles are inextricably linked. The implication is crystal clear. The leaders people admire are ones who have the *courage of their convictions.* They expect their leaders to have values, but it's even more essential that these leaders are willing to stand up for their beliefs during times of intense challenge and radical change.

What gets *you* going in the morning, eager to embrace whatever might be in store for the day? What motivates *you* to do your best, day in and day out? Why do people push their own limits to get extraordinary things done? And for that matter, why do people do many things for little or no tangible reward? Extrinsic rewards—the traditional cliché of "what gets rewarded gets done"—certainly can't explain these actions in higher education. Institutions can't pay people to care about students, alumni, or even their colleagues; they can't pay people to care about their classes, programs, services, facilities, families, or even the college's bottom line.

A sense of meaning and purpose is what gets people through the tough times, when they don't think they can even get up in the morning or take another step, give another lecture, make comments on another blue book, write another article, generate another strategic report, refurbish another residence hall, attend another pep rally, organize another reception, or hold another orientation. The motivation to deal with the challenges and uncertainties of life and work comes from the inside and not from something that others hold out as some kind of carrot. One of the primary motivating factors for Kim and her PACE team was to keep a focus on what any changes would mean to the students she worked with every day: "We do what we do to change the lives of our students," she told us. Keeping that noble transformational possibility in the forefront was central to their sustained efforts to overhaul their programs.

It's evident from our research, and from studies by many others, that if people are going to do their best, they must be *internally* motivated.[4] This is nowhere truer than in the higher-education arena. The task or project in which they're engaged must be intrinsically rewarding. When it comes to excellence, it's definitely *not* "what gets rewarded gets done"; it's "what *is rewarding* gets done." Leaders tap in to people's hearts and minds. They get faculty and staff to understand, appreciate, and believe in the noble purposes of their specific organizational unit or department within the context of the overall college's mission.

Look Outward for Fresh Ideas

When faced with new challenges, people live with a high degree of ambiguity. Change and the accompanying uncertainty throw off customary equilibrium. Yet it's these fluctuations, disturbances, and imbalances that are the primary sources of creativity.[5] Leaders must embrace innovation as they navigate their departments, programs, and institutions through what is becoming the permanent white water surrounding higher education.

Leaders appreciate that improvements and innovations can come from anywhere. For example, some of the best new ideas for classes and program changes come from alumni. Technology applications often find their way onto college campuses after first being introduced in corporations. Changes in service-learning experiences at the secondary-school level have accelerated the scale and scope of university-based initiatives. Consequently, you must be actively looking and listening to what's going on around you for even the fuzziest sign or weakest signal that there's something new on the horizon.

Being innovative requires more listening and communication than does repetitive, predictable work. Guiding a change demands that leaders establish more interpersonal relationships, connect with more sources of information, and get out of their offices—even off their own campuses—more frequently than taking care of routine responsibilities. This means you must stay in touch with trends in the academic and professional marketplaces, with the ideas and advice of people from a variety of backgrounds and disciplines, and with ongoing social, political, technological, economic, and artistic changes.

Godfrey Mungal, when he became dean, inherited a school of engineering that was in financial turmoil, with enrollments failing

to meet budget targets and donor contributions declining. To move
the school forward, one of the first orders of business was achieving
financial stability. Godfrey realized that to raise revenue, he had to
look outside the existing portfolio of degree programs. He and his
colleagues saw the possibility of offering a series of nondegree courses
and certificate programs for graduates and area professionals. For
example, they developed a series of short courses on such hot topics
as photovoltaics and renewable energy that could be taken for credit
or self-enrichment.

If leaders are going to detect opportunities for change—before
those opportunities wither, become demands, or cause huge problems—they must use their outsight. *Outsight* is the sibling of insight,
and it means being able to perceive external realities. Without outsight,
innovation cannot happen. And insight without outsight is like seeing
clearly with blinders on—you just don't get the complete picture. It can
also be useful to get outside your usual discipline or functional field.
Attend a conference in an entirely different area from your own; take
a class in a different field; tour facilities in industries with which you
are unfamiliar. See the world through a different lens.

To get a good sense of the external realities, you must get up from
your desk, get out of your office, and talk with your constituents—local
citizens, staff, employers, trustees, alumni, faculty, students, suppliers,
vendors, managers, or just interested parties. You have to listen—in
person, on the phone, via email, via websites, through social media—
and stay in touch with what is going on around you. You also need
to put yourself into new situations, which forces you to examine and
confront your existing paradigms; this is akin to gathering data and
analyzing it. Be willing to hear, consider, and accept ideas from sources
outside higher education.

For example, consider "associating," the discovery skill linked
with innovators, which involves making connections across "seemingly unrelated questions, problems, or ideas."[6] Consider how you

might stir the imagination by starting a discussion with your colleagues about such questions as: *How would Disney engage with our admissions process? How would Southwest Airlines cut our costs? How would Starbucks design our alumni relations program? How would Amazon register our students?*

EXPERIMENT AND TAKE RISKS

If we're talking about challenging the status quo, you might ask, *Why not start BIG?* Unfortunately, problems conceived of too broadly can be overwhelming. Just thinking about big problems can defeat our capacity even to imagine what might be done, let alone strengthen our desire to solve them.

Leaders face a similar challenge: that mountain (a curriculum change, or shift in parking policy, or integration of marketing practices) looks much too high and difficult to climb; even taking the first few steps can't be contemplated. Getting yourself and others to exchange old mind-sets and habits for new ways of thinking and acting is daunting. Even with the best intentions, people tend to revert to old and familiar patterns, especially in times of stress. Therefore leaders must get people to *want* to change the direction in which they're currently headed on a one-step-at-a-time basis.[7]

The most effective change processes are incremental; leaders break down big problems into small, doable steps and get the people around them to say yes numerous times, not just once. Successful leaders help others see how progress can be made by breaking down the journey into measurable goals and milestones. This was precisely the process Richard Hall, associate dean, employed when developing and launching a new executive MBA program, an education space the university had never entered.

One of the most radical things they did, which had never been done before, was to integrate faculty from a variety of fields seemingly unrelated to a business education, such as philosophy, art, and music. The faculty stumbled a lot at the beginning of the program, as did the students, in sorting out what was happening and how they were to take responsibility for integrating the lessons and learnings across the various disciplines. Richard and his team referred to the multiple iterations of faculty and student efforts as "trials" and viewed each as a learning opportunity. The program's eventual success was due to their ability to build on these trial experiences as a series of small wins. The methodology, Richard explained, was "trialing things wherever possible in bite-size chunks, on a small scale. Failing often, and failing fast, and being prepared to be as agile as we could and changing things as needed."[8]

Richard's experience illustrates that change, or learning, doesn't typically happen overnight: it's a step-by-step process. Leaders break projects, dreams, and aspirations into smaller pieces so that their constituents can make progress. An essential building block in achieving these small wins is soliciting feedback. When students volunteered to participate in trials, Richard's team would make sure everyone understood that it was an experiment and that students and faculty were required to give feedback about their experiences. That information would be forwarded to the various academic committees, and they would make any necessary adjustments.

Reflecting on the experience, Richard said, "So you do it small scale, you make sure it's a trial, you take the feedback very seriously, and you spend a lot of time deliberating about what worked and what didn't. And then you try it again and again."

Whether it was a success or a failure, Richard's team constantly monitored what they were doing while they were doing it and after they had done it. He went on to explain: "We have an informal debrief, a more formal debrief, a formal debrief that involves the full evaluation, the final evaluation, and then the preliminary for the next delivery. We revisit that again, looking at the changes that are being made and planned as we go to the next time we deliver it. That is time-consuming, but that's part and parcel of a constantly evolving program."

The academic community has always understood that major breakthroughs are likely the result of the work of scores of researchers, as countless contributions finally add up to a solution. Advances in medicine or biophysics, for example, often involve many experiments focused on various pieces of the problem. Likewise, taking the sum total—all the "little" improvements in technology regardless of the industry—has contributed to a more substantial increase in organizational productivity than all the great inventors and their inventions.[9] Progress is more likely the result of a focus on incremental improvements in tools and processes than of tectonic shifts of minds. Leaders keep the dream in mind, then they act and adapt on the move.

Make Small Wins Work

This incremental change process that leaders like Richard use has been called "small wins," as each success enables leaders to build people's commitment to a course of action.[10] The alumni or development office does much the same thing when they ask graduating students and recent alumni for a small contribution. They know that it's easier to go back and request more in the future from those who've made an initial pledge than to return to someone who's never made a contribution. Leaders start with actions that are within their control, that are tangible, that are doable, and that can get the ball rolling.

The small-wins process may not have initially been on Jeanne Rosenberger's mind as the dean of student life at a small private non-secular university, but she put it to good use when she found herself as the link between the administration and a student group protesting the university's acceptance of a major donation from a government defense contractor. Jeanne needed to find a way to keep the protest from escalating, to ensure everyone's safety, to safeguard the health of the students who decided to fast as part of their protest, and to formulate a win-win outcome.

Jeanne aimed to cultivate a calm, collaborative setting rather than a confrontational one. This she managed step by step, gaining agreements and trust from multiple parties along the way. She made sure that a neutral location was used for meetings, emphasizing the importance of face-to-face communication and careful listening. She began each conversation with the students by asking about their health and well-being—not with any ultimatums. She gained their trust by promising that the university would call the police or campus safety department only if needed, rather than having a constant police presence.

As a result, the protest remained peaceful, the students fasted for four days—with no health problems—and a dialogue about the development of a corporate gift policy for the institution began. If Jeanne had not taken the small-wins approach and had instead seen the situation as an enormous problem, the protest could have escalated and resulted in a disaster. But it didn't. Jeanne realized that incremental steps were the most promising path to a successful resolution. Afterward she made use of this experience to involve students in reflecting on what they had learned—about the demonstration, about the university, about corporations, and about themselves. Turning a protest into a learning opportunity—a teachable moment—required being open about the process and made it a win for everyone.

Small wins form the basis for a consistent pattern of accomplishment that attracts people who want to be allied with a successful venture. Small wins build people's confidence and reinforce their natural desire to feel successful. Because additional resources tend to flow to winners, slightly larger steps or wins can be attempted next. A series of small wins therefore provides a foundation of stable building blocks. Each win preserves gains and makes it harder to return to preexisting conditions; each win also offers information that facilitates learning and adaptation.

Small wins also deter opposition for a simple reason: it's hard to argue against success. Thus small wins decrease resistance to subsequent proposals. In achieving a small win, you identify the place to get started. You make the project seem doable and within existing skill and resource levels. This approach minimizes the cost of trying and reduces the risk of failing. With the achievement of a small win, natural forces are set in motion, propelling actions toward another small win. This simple strategy of winning step-by-step succeeds more often than massive overhauls and gigantic projects. It's not just that it's easier; it's also because personal and group commitment is built in to the process.

Learn from Mistakes

There's no denying that change and leadership involve taking risks, and with any uncertain action there are always, at a minimum, mistakes and, worse yet, failures. To be sure, failure can be costly. For the individual who leads a failed project, it can mean a stalled career or even a lost job. For the scholar, pursuing a new avenue of research may result in failure to receive tenure or a promotion. For the institute or center, it can lead to a loss of contracts and funding. For a dean or college president, it can mean a vote of no confidence.

It is, however, absolutely essential to take risks. On the academic side, all scholarship, with its scientific method of hypothesis testing, is an experiment in risk-taking (with the goal of explaining variance or the unknown). On the staff side, few programs have ever become better by not doing anything different. Over and over again, people in our studies tell us how mistakes, setbacks, and even failures have played a role in their successes. Without those experiences, there would have been little to no learning, and they would have been unable to achieve their aspirations or discover breakthrough achievements.

For instance, Lillas Marie Hatala, as a program director for her university's continuing education division, told us about her first encounters with the dean of the business school and how they had clashed over which of their organizational units should be offering business and leadership programs. Their discussions and negotiations often seemed to proceed, Lillas said, "one step forward and two steps back," but eventually they succeeded in working through their differences. Lillas realized that successful collaboration requires a bit of back-and-forth to formulate a shared vision, find common values, and put together a solid practical operational plan.

It may seem ironic, but many echo the thought that the overall quality of work improves when people have a chance to be tested—and possibly even fail. Whatever the endeavor, a learning curve has never been a straight line. In fact, most innovations could be called "failures in the middle." In any new endeavor, you seldom learn without making mistakes. Consider the times when you tried to learn a new sport or game. Maybe it was skiing, snowboarding, surfing, skateboarding, tennis, golf, hockey, bridge, or the latest video game. It's highly unlikely that you got it perfect on the very first try.

Nothing is ever done perfectly the first time—not in sports, not in games, and most certainly not in higher education. The point isn't to promote failure for failure's sake, of course. We don't advocate for a moment that failure ought to be the *objective* of an endeavor. Instead we advocate learning. Resilience is built through the process of learning from mistakes and setbacks. Leaders don't give up easily on themselves or others, and when things don't work out as expected they view the outcome as temporary, local, and changeable.

Exemplary leaders do not look for someone to blame when mistakes are made in the name of innovation. Instead they ask, *What can be learned from the experience?* That was certainly the approach Lillas took in her negotiations with the dean, and the data supports this perspective. The extent to which leaders were reported "Asking 'What can we learn?' when things don't go as expected" was significantly (p < 0.001) related to the level of commitment to the organization expressed by their direct reports.

There is no simple test for determining the best tactic for learning. But it is clear that leaders approach each new and unfamiliar experience with a willingness to learn, an appreciation for the importance of learning, and a recognition that learning, inescapably, involves making some mistakes.

There is likewise no simple test for ascertaining the appropriate level of risk in a new venture. Costs, benefits, potential losses and gains—all must be weighed. Knowing that one person's risk is another's routine activity, you must factor in the present skills of your team members and the demands of the task. But even if you could compute risk to the fifth decimal place, every innovation would still expose you to some peril. Perhaps the healthiest thing anyone can do is complete a risk assessment and determine whether what can be learned is worth the cost.

Promote Psychological Hardiness

Uncertainty and risk come along with any effort to make matters better and improve on the status quo. But how are leaders able to accept the inevitable mistakes, setbacks, and even failures—and the accompanying stress—associated with leadership? How do you help others handle the stress of change? It turns out that it isn't the stress that makes people ill; it's how they view and respond to stressful events.

The Personal-Best Leadership Experiences shared with us—like the campus protest Jeanne faced or handing over the conference reins to the students as Jackie did—are clear examples of difficult, stressful projects that generated enthusiasm and enjoyment. Instead of being debilitated by the stress of a challenging experience, in relating their personal bests people generally said they were energized by them. That was certainly the case with Karen Slakey Hull when she assumed responsibility for the university's reproduction and graphics services department. There were large operating deficits, and reserves had been depleted. The equipment was obsolete, production volumes were low, spoilage was excessive, print quality was not up to modern standards, and customer satisfaction was suffering. Employees worked hard but feared for their jobs and were skeptical of leadership's ability to make the required changes.

None of this deterred Karen. "I was an experienced business-woman and not an expert in the print, copy, or graphic design business," she told us. "But I was confident that together with the employees the situation could be turned around." Karen and the management staff evaluated each product and service. They looked at revenue/expense relationships, customer demand, product quality, and the type and quantity of work that was being outsourced. They conducted a customer satisfaction survey and learned what was really important to consumers.

Upgraded equipment required new, higher-level skills. To ease the transition, production staff attended conferences on state-of-the-art production equipment and processes and also received extensive training specific to the new machines. Karen and her managers coached staff in their new roles while also recognizing employees who continued to work on traditional printing presses. Throughout this time Karen held monthly all-staff meetings so that teams could present their unit updates, including major achievements and near-term goals.

Karen, her managers, and the staff could have given up in the difficult situation they faced. But they didn't. They stepped up to the challenge and overcame it. This is precisely what researchers refer to as "grit."[11] *Grit* is an individual's ability to maintain passion and persevere despite a lack of positive feedback. The characteristic *forward-looking*, which we identified earlier as an important quality for leaders, provides leaders with an enduring focus on long-term outcomes. Research shows that grittiness is associated with those individuals who most often Challenge the Process.[12]

Moreover, the ability to grow and thrive in stressful, risk-abundant situations, such as the one that Karen and her colleagues faced, is highly dependent on how you view change. Psychologists, intrigued by people who experience a high degree of stress and yet are able to cope with it positively, have discovered that these individuals have a distinctive attitude toward stress, which they call "psychological hardiness."[13] Researchers over the past 40 years have found that in groups as diverse as corporate managers, entrepreneurs, students, nurses, lawyers, and combat soldiers, those high in psychological hardiness are much more likely to withstand serious challenges and bounce back from failure than those low in hardiness.[14] And the good news is that hardiness is an attitude that people can learn and that leaders can support.

There are three key beliefs to being psychologically hardy: *commitment, control,* and *challenge.* All were evident in Karen's personal-best leadership case study. To turn adversity into advantage, first you need to commit yourself to what's happening. You have to get involved, engaged, and curious. You can't sit back and wait for something to happen. When you commit, you find in whatever you are doing something that seems interesting, meaningful, or worthwhile. You also have to take control of your own life. You need to attempt to influence what is going on. While all of your attempts may not be successful, you can't sink into powerlessness or passivity or victimhood. You can't engage in denial or feel disengaged, bored, and empty. Finally, if you are going to be psychologically hardy, you need to view challenge as an opportunity to learn from both negative and positive experiences. You can't play it safe. Personal improvement and fulfillment come through the continual process of being engaged in the uncertainties of life. Easy comfort and security are not only unrealistic but also potentially stultifying.

Your view of events contributes to your ability to cope with change and stress. To take that first step, to start that new project, and to initiate improvement, you have to believe, like Karen, that you can influence the outcome of the situation. You have to be curious about whatever is going on. You have to look for learning every step of the way. With a hardy attitude, you can transform stressful events into positive opportunities for growth and renewal.

What's more, you can help your team feel the same way. For example, when Karen asked the production manager for a proposal to modernize the equipment, he came back with a five-year plan. Karen asked, "What would happen if we made this investment in one year?" His eyes opened wide in an expression that said, *Wow, we really could change this place!* He returned with a one-year plan that made strategic and financial sense.

People with a hardy attitude take change, risk, turmoil, and the strains of life in stride. Whether the stressful event they encounter is positive or negative, they react similarly. They consider the incident engaging, believe they have the capacity and capability to influence the outcome, and see it as an opportunity for learning and development.

You can't enlist and retain people if you don't cultivate an atmosphere that promotes psychological hardiness. Given alternatives, people won't remain long with a cause that distresses them. To accept the challenge of change, they need to believe that they can overcome adversity. You can help the people you work with cope more effectively by promoting conditions in which people experience commitment rather than alienation, control rather than powerlessness, and challenge rather than threat. For example, provide and assign tasks that are challenging but within the person's skill set and that help build their sense of control. Offering rewards and recognition rather than punishment fosters commitment. Encouraging people to see how change can generate a range of possibilities promotes an attitude of adaptability.

It's instructive to know that people associate doing their best with feelings of meaningfulness, mastery, and stimulation, and people are biased in the direction of hardiness when thinking about their best. It's equally helpful to know that people don't produce excellence when feeling uninvolved, insignificant, and threatened. Furthermore, feelings of commitment, control, and challenge provide internal cues for recognizing when you are excelling as opposed to only making it through the day.

QUESTIONS FOR REFLECTION: *CHALLENGE THE PROCESS*

The quest for change is an adventure. It tests your skills and abilities and awakens talents that have been dormant. It's the training ground for leadership. Exemplary leaders search for opportunities to make a difference—even when those opportunities are sometimes thrust upon them rather than chosen. You need to remain diligent for anything that lulls your department or program into a false sense of security; constantly invite and launch new initiatives. You need to be out in front of change, not behind it trying to catch up. The focus of your attention should be less on the routine operations and much more on the untried and untested. Ask, "What's new? What's next? What's better?" That's where the future is.

Leaders experiment and learn from their mistakes. One of your major leadership tasks involves identifying and removing self-imposed constraints and organizational conventions that block innovation and creativity. Yet innovation is always risky, and you must recognize failure as a fact of experimental life. Instead of punishing it, encourage it; instead of fixing blame for mistakes, learn from them; instead of adding rules, promote flexibility. Embrace continuous improvement and lifelong learning.

Leaders have a hardy attitude about change. Venture outside the constraints of your normal routine and experiment with creative possibilities. Foster climates in which faculty and staff alike can accept the challenge of becoming better. By having and fostering an attitude of psychological hardiness, you can turn the potential turmoil and stress of innovation and evolution into an adventure. Set the stage by getting started, taking the first step, and achieving small wins.

In developing your competence in the leadership practice of Challenge the Process, spend some time reflecting on the following questions. After you've given them sufficient consideration, let others know what you are thinking and willing to do.

▶ What are the experiments or pilot projects you are engaged in or sponsoring in your department or unit? Are these sufficient? How are you going to evaluate not just the outcomes but the learning?

▶ What can you do to ensure that people in your group feel that you have their backs and are supporting them as they exercise outsight and take initiative to be innovative and try new ideas? What more could you be doing?

▶ What will it take for you to say yes more often than you are now? What can you do to make it easy for others to say yes and undertake something they have never done before?

▶ When things don't go as expected, what can you do to adopt a learning perspective on the outcome or process? How can you demonstrate your willingness to take ownership of your foibles and missteps?

CHAPTER 5

Enable Others to Act

CAROLYN BORNE IS PROGRAM DIRECTOR of the Women's Health Initiative in a well-known medical school at a large state university. Part of a National Institutes of Health project, the Women's Health Initiative is one of the largest and most ambitious longitudinal studies of postmenopausal women's health concerns ever undertaken. The study requires careful planning, analytical ability, and meticulous attention to detail.

Because of its sensitive and significant nature, it also requires that the staff members have a high degree of collaboration and trust. But that climate didn't exist when Carolyn arrived. The emphasis seemed to be on competition and suspicion rather than cooperation and support. Hard as the staff members were working, they were not at the expected national study goal for recruitment. Productivity and morale were low.

Carolyn took immediate steps to establish a different kind of climate, where people felt they knew one another and were respected and trusted by their colleagues. In the process of completing a needs assessment, she interviewed each staff member. She found that while people were enthusiastic about the study, they were frustrated by the lack of systems, organization, and especially teamwork; in fact, she said, "Each member of the team was a talented professional, but each was ready to quit. They all liked their jobs but did not feel supported."

Carolyn set a goal to increase group cohesion through improving communication, making connections, and facilitating relationships. As Carolyn told us, "We started creating a team environment with a daylong retreat, at which we began to identify our values, philosophy, and mission. We shared stories about families and loved ones and began to feel a sense of trust and respect for each other." Carolyn understood that to create a climate of collaboration and trust, she needed to determine what the group members needed, build the team around mutual respect and a common purpose, and make each team member strong and efficacious.

In the thousands of leadership cases we've studied, like Carolyn's, we've yet to encounter a single example of leadership that's occurred without the leader's actively involving and relying on the support and contributions of other people. Likewise, we haven't found a single instance in which encouraging competition was the way to achieve the highest levels of performance. Quite the contrary, when at their personal best as leaders, people spoke passionately about teamwork and cooperation as the interpersonal route to success, especially when the conditions were urgent and extremely challenging. They understood that their fundamental leadership challenge was creating an environment in which people on their team, in the department, or with the program could do their work collaboratively. These leaders knew that for others to act at their best, they needed to trust one another.

The most effective leaders in higher education are those who most frequently Enable Others to Act. We asked direct reports how often their leaders engaged in the six behaviors associated with Enable Others to Act on the *Leadership Practices Inventory*, with assessments ranging from 1 (Almost never) to 10 (Almost always). We also asked them a separate question about the extent to which they agreed or disagreed with the statement *Overall, this person is an effective leader*

(1 = Strongly disagree and 5 = Strongly agree). The analysis showed that the effectiveness ratings of leaders by their direct reports increased systematically ($p < 0.001$) as leaders were observed engaging more and more frequently in the behaviors associated with enabling others to act. There was a 40 percent bump in effectiveness from the bottom to the top quartile.

CREATE A CLIMATE OF TRUST

Leaders put trust-building on their agendas; they don't leave it to chance. It's *the* central issue in human relationships within and outside organizations. Without trust you cannot lead. Individuals who are unable to trust others fail to become leaders precisely because they can't bear to be dependent on the words and work of others. So they either end up doing all the work themselves or supervise work so closely that they become over-controlling micromanagers. Because they don't trust other people, the result is that those people don't trust them in return.

Psychologists find that individuals who are capable of trusting people are happier and more psychologically adjusted than those who view the world with suspicion and distrust.[1] Trusting individuals are also liked more by their peers and often sought out as friends. You listen more to those you trust and more readily accept their influence. The most effective leadership situations are those in which each member of the team trusts the leader, as well as one another.

Picture your faculty colleagues in a department meeting, your administrative colleagues in a program review meeting, or even a campuswide task force or governance committee. Now imagine that these people are involved in a role-playing exercise. They are given identical factual information about a tough policy decision (such as program budget cuts) and then asked to solve a problem related to that information as a group. Half of the groups are briefed to expect trusting behavior ("You have learned from your past experiences that you can trust the other members in your group and can openly express feelings and differences with them"); the other half are primed to expect untrusting behavior. Will you be surprised that there will be substantial differences in the ways the members of these two groups interact and problem-solve with one another?

Studies such as this one consistently show that the group members who were told they could trust their role-playing peers and manager reported that their discussion and decisions were significantly more positive on *every* factor measured than did the members of the low-trust group. Members of the high-trust group were more open about their feelings, experienced greater clarity about the group's problems and goals, and searched for more alternative courses of action. They also reported greater influence on outcomes, satisfaction with the meeting, motivation to implement decisions, and closeness as a team as a result of the meeting.

In another simulation, participants were told that, based on past experiences, their manager could always be trusted or could not always be trusted. In those groups in which the manager was not to be trusted, people ignored or distorted genuine attempts by the manager to be open and honest. Distrust was so strong that members viewed the manager's candor as a clever attempt to deceive them and reacted by sabotaging the manager's efforts even further. Managers who experienced rejection of their attempts to be trusting and open responded in kind. Not surprisingly, more than two-thirds of the participants in the low-trust group said they would give serious consideration to looking for another position. People don't want to work with people or in settings where there is little trust.[2]

It's crucial to keep in mind that the incidents reported above actually occurred, but they were *a simulation;* the participants were role-playing! People behaved and responded as they did as a consequence of being *told* that they couldn't trust one another. Their actions demonstrated that trust or distrust can come with a mere suggestion—and in minutes. Trust, quite simply, is a significant predictor of individuals' satisfaction with their organizations.

You show that you trust people when you listen to them and provide opportunities for them to contribute freely, make choices, and be innovative. You demonstrate trust when you nurture openness, involvement, personal satisfaction, and high levels of commitment to excellence. Knowing that trust is essential, make sure that you consider alternative viewpoints, draw on other people's expertise and abilities, and let others exercise influence over group decisions. People need to believe that they can rely on you to do what's in everyone's best interests. The feeling of *we* cannot happen without trust.

While trust is a reciprocal process, as the leader you have to be the one who antes up first. "Why should I trust my supervisor," one library staff member told us, "when she doesn't ever seem to trust me?" This sentiment was echoed by many people across campuses and was especially telling in hierarchical relationships. When the manager says, "Trust me," but doesn't by her actions demonstrate that she trusts others, or doesn't take the time to listen and be open to being influenced, trust doesn't blossom or flourish. Trust begets trust. The truth is that trust comes first; following comes second.

Facilitate Positive Interdependence and Cooperation

Millions of people have tuned in over the years to watch the "reality" show *Survivor*. With its competitive games, petty rivalries, backstabbing betrayals, tribal councils, and cliffhanger endings, the show has survived 38 seasons and counting. It's been ranked among the "best series of all times," and both faculty and staff alike have sometimes suggested that the show is a case study in how to be successful in any organizational setting.

To us this conclusion is troubling, and we take strong exception to any real-life application. Riveting or not, *Survivor* and shows like it teach all the wrong lessons about how to survive in the "real world."

In the real world, let alone in higher education, if people were to behave as these players on television did, they'd all be dead. As the acclaimed anthropologist Lionel Tiger put it, "The contest format distorted savagely what would have otherwise been a very different outcome involving ongoing cooperation. The behavior on the island… is a reflection of the nature of the prize, and what winning it demanded. The goal of human survival has always been to endure for another day, and in the group."[3]

One of the most significant aspects of cooperation and collaboration missing from *Survivor* is a sense of interdependence, a condition under which everyone knows that they cannot succeed unless everyone else succeeds—or at least that they can't succeed unless they coordinate their efforts. If there is no sense of *We are all in this together*, that the success of one depends on the success of the others, it's virtually impossible to set the conditions for positive teamwork.

The motivation for working diligently on your own job, keeping in mind the overall common objective, is reinforced when the end result is what gets rewarded and not the individual efforts. To make extraordinary things happen, people have to rely on one another. Leaders take an active role in creating both a positive context and a structure for cooperation and collaboration. The leaders who were reported as most often "developing cooperative relationships among the people they work with" were viewed by their direct reports, as illustrated in figure 5.1, as instilling the strongest feelings of team spirit.

This was very true in Susan Tomaro's experience when she had the challenging assignment of planning a weeklong new-student orientation program during a time that overlapped with the Jewish High Holy Days. Not only would there be conflicting events but the two activities would be competing over the use of limited campus facilities. It was her first year in this position, and she immediately went to work to build strong relationships with the Office of Religious Life and Hillel.

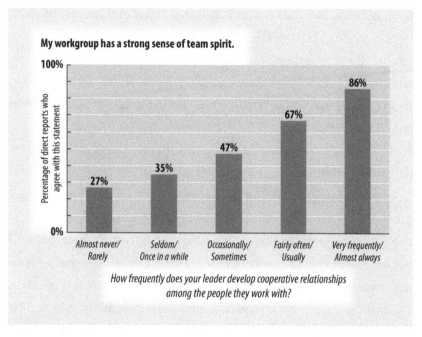

Figure 5.1 The extent that leaders are viewed as developing cooperative relationships among the people they work with increases team spirit in their work groups.

Susan understood that she would not be able to argue that her program was more important than these religious holidays to those involved with them, nor would they be able to necessarily claim that this religiously important time trumped priority over use of the campus facilities. Susan understood that they needed to work together to resolve potential conflicts. What she did was "provide information about the various challenges we all faced and seek everyone's help to change the way we would do things this time around. I asked people on all sides to think outside the box and recognize that the issues could be resolved only by getting many people involved and working together. Nobody was going to be successful without the support of everyone working together with one another." A zero-sum solution would not be to anyone's benefit.

Leaders, like Susan, appreciate that collaboration results from people understanding that they have to rely and depend on one another for their mutual success. With this realization, asking for help and sharing information comes naturally. Because they see themselves in a mutually beneficial relationship, finding and setting a common goal is not problematic.

Charlie Slater also understood the importance of positive inter-dependence and collaboration when talking about his Personal-Best Leadership Experience. In the successful development and imple-mentation of the university's first doctoral program, Charlie told us that "there were many leaders" and that this accomplishment would not have been possible "without the leadership and cooperation of so many people." Everyone was willing to cooperate with one another, assuming complementary roles to move the possibility into reality. The university's president started the ball rolling. Charlie and a small group of faculty then worked together to advocate for the program and to keep pushing the project along. Throughout the process, different individuals and groups enabled others through advocacy, reconcilia-tion, and negotiation.

For example, a veteran faculty member came forward at a key point to lend support. By emphasizing the group's shared beliefs and couching them in moral terms, she was able to reconcile competing factions. Charlie explained that her efforts were "crucial to connect-ing the university's mission and values to the doctoral program." By helping faculty acknowledge these shared beliefs, Charlie's colleagues were able to make the time to develop a curriculum, establish learning objectives and research standards, and continue their commitment to these tasks amid other demands.

Whether it's launching a doctoral program, designing a new campus facility, changing personnel benefits, bringing updated soft-ware online, shifting financial record-keeping systems, instituting new safety procedures for science labs, or expanding public safety protocols, for people to work together as a team you have to ensure that they have a specific reason for being together and cooperating with one another. Make sure the people you are working with understand the goal they are working toward, feel a shared stake in the outcome, have an appreciation for the talents and resources individuals bring to the endeavor, and have the latitude necessary to be both imaginative and strategic. A focus on a collective purpose binds people in cooperative efforts. Shared values and visions serve this function for the long term, and group goals provide this same common focus for the shorter term. Only through shared goals and recognized interdependence in one another's success can people diligently strive to devise integrative solutions.

Support Norms of Reciprocity

A sense of mutuality is essential to a productive long-term relationship. If one party always gives and the other always takes, the one who gives will feel taken advantage of, and the one who takes will feel superior. In that climate, cooperation is virtually impossible. To forge cooperative relationships, you must establish norms of reciprocity among all parties and within teams.

The power of reciprocity is dramatically demonstrated in a well-known study generally referred to as the "prisoner's dilemma." The dilemma is that two parties (individuals or groups) are confronted with a series of situations in which they must decide whether to cooperate. They don't know in advance how the other party will behave. There are two basic strategies: cooperate (don't say anything) or compete (blame the other party); and there are four possible outcomes based on the choices players make: win-lose, lose-win, lose-lose, and win-win.

The maximum individual payoff comes when one player selects a non-cooperative strategy and the other player chooses to cooperate in good faith. In this "I win but you lose" approach, one party gains at the other's expense. Although this might seem to be the most successful strategy—at least for the non-cooperative player—it rarely proves successful in the long run mainly because the other player won't continue to cooperate in the face of the first player's non-cooperative strategy. This typically leads to both parties deciding not to cooperate and attempting to maximize their respective individual payoffs. In the end both lose. When both parties choose to cooperate, however, both win, though in the short run the personal payoff for a cooperative move (win-win) is less than what it might be for a competitive one (win-lose).

Over the years researchers have found, amazingly enough, that when faced with such dilemmas the most successful strategy in the long run is quite simple: cooperate on the first move and then do whatever the other player did on the previous move. This strategy succeeds by eliciting cooperation from others, not by defeating them.[4] Simply put, people who reciprocate are more likely to be successful than those who try to maximize individual advantage.

Dilemmas successfully solved by this strategy are by no means restricted to the prisoner's dilemma or theoretical research. You face similar dilemmas every day, both personally and professionally: *Will others take advantage of me if I'm cooperative? Will it be worth the cost for me to maximize my personal gain? How much, if at all, should I compromise my interests so that others can achieve more of theirs?*

Reciprocity turns out to be the most successful approach for such daily decisions because it demonstrates both a willingness to be cooperative and an unwillingness to be taken advantage of. As a long-term strategy, reciprocity minimizes the risk of escalation: If people know that you'll respond in kind, why would they start trouble? And if people know that you'll reciprocate, they know that the best way to deal with you is to cooperate and become beneficiaries of your cooperation. Honor codes succeed on this principle, as do goodwill gestures between public safety and campus housing, as well as negotiations between various faculty councils and their staff counterparts.

Reciprocity leads to predictability and stability, which in turn can keep relationships and negotiations from breaking down.[5] The knowledge that goals are shared and that people will reciprocate in their efforts to achieve them makes working together less stressful. Improved relationships and decreased stress are obviously fine outcomes under any circumstances.

Foster Face-to-Face Interactions

Group goals, reciprocity, and rewarding joint efforts are all essential for collaboration to occur, but positive face-to-face communication has the most powerful influence on whether intended results are achieved.[6] This need for face-to-face interaction increases with the complexity of the issues. For example, in working through many of the scheduling challenges around new-student orientation, Susan had many one-on-one discussions with key players across the campus who could help think through the issues and effect change—"enlisting their help and working collaboratively." In the end Susan told us that she became very good friends with a number of central partners, including the campus rabbi, as a consequence of these many interactions.

Look for ways you can provide frequent and lasting opportunities for team members to associate and intermingle across disciplines and between departments (or schools, colleges, programs, or divisions). As handy as virtual tools such as email, voicemail, apps, and texts are for staying in touch, they are no substitute for positive face-to-face communication. Just showing up is far more effective in building successful relationships.

One of the benefits of the leadership development program that Kelly McInnes co-created with campus leaders is that all members of the cohort each year are on the same campus, which makes it possible for collaboration and connection to continue even when the program has ended. When participants initially asked her, "What's next?" she put the responsibility back on them: "What can you do to stay together? What do you think is next?" One of the department heads in the program piped up and offered to set up a time outside their training sessions to get together at a local pub—he'd even buy the first round. "That's really all you need," Kelly said. "You just need to get them in the same space together. I can facilitate the logistics—time and place, provide a little bit of coordination. That's all you need to do to keep the relationships, and learning from shared experiences, going."

When people expect their interactions to continue into the future (e.g., they'll run into one another at some campus event, they'll continue to serve on this committee for several years, participate in a subsequent task force, attend another game or performance), they are much more likely to cooperate in the present. Knowing that you have to deal with someone in the future ensures that neither you nor they will easily forget about how you've treated one another. When future interactions are likely to be frequent, the consequences of today's actions on tomorrow's dealings are that much more pronounced. In the end, enduring relationships are more likely to produce collaboration than short-term ones, and you have every incentive as a leader to build such relationships for yourself and for the people in your department or program.

Kelly, in fact, goes out of her way to deliberately walk around her campus, not merely to enjoy its beauty but because "a big part of it is that inevitably I run into somebody that I wouldn't otherwise see. Walking around creates the possibility for these serendipitous bumps." This allows her to strike up conversations that she might not have been able to have, thereby sustaining longer-term relationships and even learning about things taking place on campus that she might not otherwise know about.

Produce Social Capital

The new currency of the information age and the IoT (Internet of Things) is not intellectual capital; it is *social capital*—the collective value of the people we know and what we'll do for one another. When social connections are strong and numerous, there's more trust, reciprocity, information flow, collective action, and even happiness.[7] Therefore part of your personal agenda should be to get connected to the sources of information, resources, and influences you will need to make a difference. Make sure you also connect your colleagues and constituents to each other and to those on the outside who are central to key networks. It will make them more effective, more engaged in critical tasks, and more satisfied with their lives and work.

The most well-connected individuals are typically those who have been most involved in many campus activities. They haven't been typecast in one discipline, pedagogy, function, administrative body, or community. They've moved in and out of a range of assignments, committees, and experiences. They know people from a wide range of departments and programs, and they have made connections across faculty, staff, and even student, alumni, and community domains. They've honed their interpersonal skills and knowledge so that they're credible to their constituents, and they've not dug themselves into a rut. Most college campuses are organized into discrete units, promoting specialization, but when it comes to leadership, you have to draw on your connections. If those connections are in only your specialty, it's likely that you'll be less influential than you could be if your connections cross a lot of boundaries. When it comes to social connections, there's a real long-term payoff in mining deep and wide.

For example, when he was dean, Douglas Farenick undertook a significant revision of the science school's document that described the assignment of faculty duties, performance standards, allocation of sabbaticals, and the like. He was well aware that any changes would require buy-in by a majority of the faculty and could not be imposed from the top down. The faculty would need to trust and endorse the dean's philosophy behind any changes. Doug used the social capital he had developed, asking six faculty members whom he had productive relationships with, and who represented both the discipline and the gender diversity of the institution, to consider the possible changes, draft the proposed revisions, and select one of their members to present the rationale to the faculty as a whole. Consequently, the policy changes came from respected faculty members who had deeper and more personal ties with the faculty as a whole than the dean did, and produced greater acceptance than any hierarchical decision would have.

In an era that is becoming more and more dependent on virtual connections, there's a temptation to believe that such connections automatically lead to better relationships and greater trust. The hitch is, there really is no such thing as *virtual* trust.[8] Virtual trust, like virtual reality, is still one step removed from the real thing. People are social animals; it is our nature to want to interact face-to-face. If this weren't true, you might as well abandon having faculty in the classroom altogether and let wireless personal digital assistants do all the teaching. Bits and bytes make for a fragile social foundation. This may sound heretical in a world driving itself more and more to depend on electronic connections, but you have to figure out how to combine and balance the benefits of technology with the social imperative of human contact. Data and information may be virtually shared, but ensuring understanding, sensitivity, knowledge, and action online or at a distance are kinks still to be worked out.

GENERATE POWER ALL AROUND

Exemplary leaders make those around them feel strong and capable. They make it possible for people to take responsibility for success—and ownership of it—by enhancing their competence and self-confidence. Exemplary leaders listen to others' ideas and act on them, involve others in important decisions, and acknowledge and give credit for others' contributions. Long before *empowerment* was written in to the popular vernacular, exemplary leaders understood how vital it was that their constituents felt proficient and effective.

Feeling powerful—literally, feeling *able*—comes from a deep sense of being in control of life. People everywhere share this inclination, and when they feel able to determine their own destiny and believe that they can mobilize the resources and support necessary to complete a task, they persist in their efforts to achieve. But when people feel that they are controlled by others and believe that they are unsupported or lack the necessary resources, they show little to no commitment to excel (although they may still have to comply). Leadership behaviors that increase another's sense of self-confidence, self-determination, and personal effectiveness make that individual more powerful and greatly enhance the possibility of their achieving success. Gallup surveys involving millions of people around the world decidedly show that the extent to which people feel powerful and engaged in their work is directly linked to positive organizational outcomes, such as productivity, commitment, and retention.[9]

Creating a climate on campus where people are involved and feel important is at the heart of strengthening others. Correspondingly, you have to provide them with the latitude to make decisions based on what they believe should be done. You must provide an environment both that builds their ability to perform a task or complete an assignment and that promotes a sense of self-confidence in their judgment. People must experience a sense of personal accountability so that they can own their achievements. Exemplary leaders help others learn new skills and develop their existing talents, as well as provide the institutional supports required for ongoing growth and change. In the final analysis, you are turning your constituents, the people you work with, into leaders.

Ensure Self-Leadership

Leaders accept and act on this paradox: *You become most powerful when you give your own power away.* This is precisely the realization that Mark Delucchi shared in his Personal-Best Leadership Experience, which arose in connection with a Habitat for Humanity Collegiate Challenge. Quite simply, Mark gave students the power and the authority to carry out their assignments and jobs: "Although I tried to instill in them what I thought was important, I had them articulate what it was they wanted from this experience. I gave them the space and resources to achieve the goals as they defined them." Mark took this approach not simply with the group but with each individual. For example, when the student coordinator came to him with a question, Mark's response was, "It's your show. What do *you* want to do?" Mark encouraged people to run with their ideas and to see what they came up with. If something went wrong, "I was right there to help them learn and then move on."

Traditional thinking promotes the archaic idea that power is a fixed sum: *If I have more, you have less.* Naturally, people with this view hold tightly to the power that they perceive is theirs and are extremely reluctant to share it with anyone. This notion is wrongheaded and inconsistent with all the evidence on high-performing organizations. As Mark found out, he didn't lose any influence with the group or on the project because "it really was their show." Being a leader, Mark explained, "requires you to give up something. By giving some of the responsibility to others, they become invested and passionate about the project. Then my job becomes finding ways to help them see how it all comes together. But you've got to believe in the capabilities of your team to make this work."

From her experience in higher education, especially as the university's training and organizational development director, Lori Ann Roth seconded Mark's experience: "It's not really about giving your power away," Lori explained. "What you are giving is an opportunity for people to make their *own* 'power'—not giving them power per se but giving them an opportunity to create, to make decisions, and to feel that they are in control."

Research solidly backs up Lori's and Mark's viewpoint. Researchers have found that the more people believe that they have some degree of influence and control in their organization, greater organizational effectiveness and member satisfaction follow. Shared power results in higher job fulfillment and performance throughout the organization.[10]

When you make other people powerful, in both tangible and intangible ways, you are demonstrating profound trust in and respect for their abilities. When leaders help others grow and develop, that help is reciprocated. People who feel capable of influencing their leaders are more strongly attached to those leaders and more committed to effectively carrying out their responsibilities.[11] They *own* their jobs, feeling and accepting accountability for their actions and results and being compelled in many ways to not let their leaders' expectations and trust in them dissipate.

Provide Choices

If you desire higher levels of performance and greater initiative, you must be proactive in designing work that allows people choice in what they do. In other words, they need to have *discretion;* that means being able to take nonroutine action, exercise independent judgment, and make decisions that affect how they do their work without having to check with someone else.

The deliberations and decisions that Charlie Slater had to deal with in developing that new doctoral program were far from routine. He made sure that any proposal he brought forth to various constituency groups (like the faculty senate) provided them with options from which to choose about how the program would be introduced and shaped. He did the same for the first group of students who were actually enrolled in the program before its formal launch. In developing an alternative spring break, Kent Koth made sure that while everyone had the same "big picture" in mind, students had lots of choices about how they would structure their daily activities, both individually and collectively.

In these ways leaders, like Charlie and Kent, foster not only a sense of but also *actual* ownership among those who will be responsible for the program or project's success and vitality. Choice fuels people's sense of power and control over their lives, and the data backs up this claim. The sense of feeling highly productive dramatically increased the more often people reported that their leaders "give people a great deal of freedom and choice in deciding how to do their work," as shown in figure 5.2.

You want people to take the initiative and be self-directed. You want them to think for themselves and not continually ask, "What

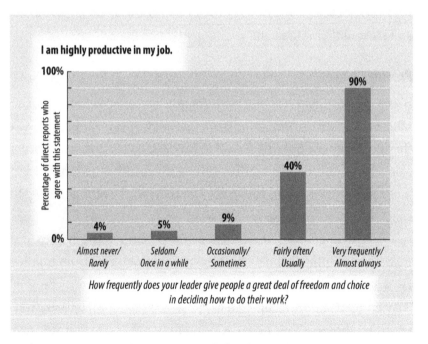

Figure 5.2 Leaders viewed as giving people freedom and choice in deciding how to do their work increase direct reports' sense of being productive.

should I do?" This ability cannot be developed if you constantly tell people what to do and how to do it. They really can't learn to act independently unless they get to exercise some degree of autonomy. If they have no freedom of choice and can operate only in ways prescribed by the organization, how can they respond when a student, alumnus, or colleague behaves in ways that aren't in the script?

If people have to ask the "bosses" what to do—even when they know what needs doing and feel they can do it—this process slows down the entire organization. And if their bosses don't know, they will have to ask their managers, and up the organizational ladder it goes. The only way to have an efficient and effective organization is by giving people the power to use their best judgment in applying their knowledge and skills. Doing so is an explicit exercise in trust.

As necessary as choice is, it is insufficient. Without the knowledge, skills, information, and resources to do a job expertly—and without feeling competent to effectively execute the choices that it requires—people feel overwhelmed and disabled. This means you'll need to ensure that you've prepared them to make these choices and that you've educated them in the guiding principles of the organization. Even when people have the resources, however, there may be times when they aren't sure they're allowed to use them or that they will be backed up if things don't go as well as expected.

Build Competence and Confidence

People can't do what they don't know how to do. So, when you increase your constituents' latitude and discretion, you also have to increase expenditures on training and development, as well as provide opportunities to learn on the job. People may be reluctant to exercise their judgment, in part because they aren't sure about how to perform critical tasks and possibly out of fear of making mistakes. Research on "Great Place to Work" companies illustrates that "ensuring that employees are given the training they need and involving them in decisions that impact their work creates both competence and commitment."[12]

Strengthening others requires upfront investments in initiatives that develop people's competencies and foster their confidence. Leaders know that if people are to feel strong, they must be continuously improving and developing their skills and abilities. Leaders know that they need to share information and resources with constituents. The confidence to do well is critical in the process of strengthening others. Just because individuals know *how* to do something doesn't necessarily mean that they *will* do it.

Faced with a lack of skills in some of the admissions office staff, Holly Wang made time to work alongside each team member, showing and talking with them about how to handle various situations. When a critical issue arose, she quickly brought the entire team together and walked them through her thought processes on how to address the dispute and fix the problem—with the clear expectation that the next time they could handle it on their own. She also set up temporary partnerships in which each partner got to know the other better, and this cross-training helped develop both partners' skills. Along with more confidence came better understanding and trust in each other. Educating, training, and coaching the other team members built self-confidence, and Holly's team became even stronger.

Enabling others to act is not just a practice. It's a crucial step in a psychological process that affects intrinsic needs for self-determination. To experience some sense of order and stability in their lives, all people have an internal need to influence other people and life's events. Leaders take actions and create conditions that strengthen their constituents' self-esteem and inner sense of effectiveness. Feeling confident that they can cope with events and situations puts people in a position to exercise leadership.

Without sufficient self-confidence, people lack the conviction necessary to take on tough challenges. The absence of self-assurance manifests itself in feelings of helplessness, powerlessness, and crippling self-doubt. Building self-confidence involves developing people's inner strength to plunge ahead in uncharted terrain, to make tough choices, to face opposition, and to meet surprises serenely because they believe in their skills and decision-making abilities.

Empirical studies document how self-confidence can affect people's performance. In one study participants were told that deci-sion-making was a skill developed through practice. The more they worked at it, the more capable they became. Another group of partici-pants was told that decision-making reflected their basic intellectual aptitude. The higher their underlying cognitive capacities, the better their decision-making ability would be.

Both groups worked with a series of problems in a simulated organization. Participants who believed that decision-making was an acquirable skill continued to set challenging goals for themselves, used good problem-solving strategies, and fostered organizational productivity. Their counterparts who believed that decision-making ability was inherent (that is, you either have it or you don't), lost con-fidence in themselves as they encountered difficulties. They lowered their aspirations for the organization, their problem-solving deterio-rated, and organizational productivity declined. Interestingly, those participants who lost confidence in their own judgment tended to find fault not so much with themselves as with their people, and they were quite uncharitable toward others, regarding them as unmotivated and unworthy of supervisory attention.[13]

As these studies—and probably your own experience—under-score, having confidence and believing in your ability to handle the job, no matter how difficult, is essential to promoting and sustain-ing consistent efforts. Fostering self-efficacy is not a warmed-over version of the power of positive thinking. Leaders communicate their belief that people can be successful. This sentiment was evident in people's Personal-Best Leadership Experiences: someone believed in them and gave them the chance to make something extraordinary happen. Knowing that someone expected them to succeed motivated them to extend themselves and to persevere in the face of any hardships or setbacks.

Foster Personal Responsibility and Accountability

Accountability is a critical element in every collaborative effort. When people take personal responsibility and are held accountable for their actions, their colleagues will be considerably more inclined to want to work with them and be generally more cooperative. Everyone has to do their part for a group to function effectively. Personal accountability is enhanced when you structure a situation so that people have to work collaboratively with one another. Knowing that your peers are expecting you to be prepared and to do your job is a powerful force in motivating people to do well. The feeling of not wanting to let the rest of the group down strengthens people's resolve to do their best. Additionally, the more people believe that everyone else is competent and taking responsibility for their own part of the job, the more trusting and cooperative they're going to be. It's also true that people will be more committed to doing their part when they are confident that others will be doing theirs.

When you explicitly give people the freedom to make choices, you are implicitly increasing the degree of personal responsibility they must necessarily accept. The interconnectedness between choice and accountability takes on increasing importance in virtually linked global workplaces. As Holly's Personal-Best Leadership Experience revealed, to foster accountability she needed to delegate authority and give others a chance to take ownership. She realized that by trusting others with responsibility, she was letting them know that she believed in them and had confidence in their abilities and judgment. Given the level of trust Holly demonstrated in them, they in turn felt greater motivation to follow through on their commitments. When you allow others to take on more responsibility, you also benefit by being freed up to take on new duties and learning opportunities yourself.

Some people are reluctant to share power because they contend that cooperative endeavors minimize individual accountability. They think that if people are encouraged to work collectively, somehow they'll take less responsibility for their own actions than if they are encouraged to compete or to do things on their own. Some people, it's true, will become social loafers, slacking off while others do their jobs for them. But that doesn't last long because their team members will quickly tire of carrying the extra load. Either the shirker steps up to the responsibility or the team wants that person out. Part of your job is to set up conditions that enable each and every team member to feel a sense of ownership for a successful outcome.

QUESTIONS FOR REFLECTION: *ENABLE OTHERS TO ACT*

You can't do it alone is the mantra of exemplary leaders—and for good reason. You just can't make a difference all by yourself. Fostering collaboration enables departments, programs, schools, and other alliances to function effectively. Collaboration can be sustained only when you promote a sense of mutual reliance—the feeling that *We are all in this together.* Common goals and roles contribute to mutual interdependence. Knowing that others will reciprocate is the best incentive for helping others achieve their goals. Help begets help just as trust begets trust. Focusing on what's to be gained fosters agreement in what might otherwise be divisive issues. Create a trusting climate by the example you set. Make sure that key constituents are able to make human contact with one another. Work to make these interactions durable and connect people to multiple sources of influence and information.

Leaders turn their constituents into leaders—making people capable of acting on their own initiative. You strengthen others when you enable them to exercise choice and discretion, when you develop in them the competence and confidence to act and to excel, and when you foster the accountability and responsibility that compels action. Exemplary leaders use their power and influence in service of others because they know that capable and confident people perform best.

In developing your competence in the leadership practice of Enable Others to Act, spend some time reflecting on the following questions. After you've given them sufficient consideration, let others know what you are thinking and willing to do.

- ▶ How can you provide people with an opportunity to grow, develop, and stretch in their jobs? Where can you empower people to take on more responsibility and accountability?

- ▶ What can you do to share more information and responsibility with people in your group? How can you keep them more informed and in the loop about what's going on outside the boundaries of your unit or function?

- ▶ Where can you make connections for your team with others in the larger institution—and in doing so provide new experiences? How can you connect people outside your group with people on your own team?

- ▶ How can you demonstrate your belief that people can learn, innovate, and make even more of a difference? Where can they exercise more latitude and discretion than they currently are?

Encourage the Heart

W HEN JENNIFER NUTEFALL AND HER UNIVERSITY LIBRARY STAFF completed their five-year strategic plan in three years, she wanted to showcase the team's accomplishments for public recognition. The library management group put together an application to the Association of College and Research Libraries, focusing on how they assessed their work, their engagement with the community, and how the organizational structure had transformed. They received an Excellence in Academic Libraries award, and, as Jennifer said, "It was a nice encapsulation of what we were able to achieve. Looking at it put together, it was really amazing.

"What's great about this award," Jennifer continued, "beyond a plaque and a modest financial reward for the library, was the opportunity for everyone to really celebrate together." Her institution planned a large celebration at which Jennifer had the chance to demonstrate just how far the library had come from the stagnant leadership practices of the past: "I wanted the campus to see, *This is who we are now. The old library you knew doesn't exist anymore.*" This public recognition was an opportunity to acknowledge how hard her staff had worked over the years to overhaul the library and overcome its challenges. She arranged for her staff members to receive library-branded fleece jackets, and she held a smaller, library-specific commemoration so that everyone could see and hold the actual award. She also assembled bound copies of the application that had won the award so that everyone who worked in the library had a physical symbol of all their hard work over the past three years. Bringing everyone together, Jennifer said, "is a really nice moment to stop and say, 'Look at what we've accomplished.'"

Like so many other leaders with whom we talked, Jennifer understood the importance of recognizing people for who they are and celebrating what they contribute and accomplish. Time and again in their personal-best leadership case studies, people reported working very intensely and for very long hours—and enjoying it. Yet to persist for months at such a pace, people need encouragement, and exemplary leaders are always there to help people find the courage they need to do things that they have never done before.

Leaders give heart to others by recognizing individual contributions and celebrating victories together. Most people rate "having a caring boss" even higher than they value money or fringe benefits. In fact, how long employees stay at a company, and how productive they are there, is determined more by the relationship they have with their immediate supervisor than by any other factor.[1]

The most effective leaders in higher education are those who most frequently Encourage the Heart. We asked direct reports how often their leaders engaged in the six behaviors associated with Encourage the Heart on the *Leadership Practices Inventory,* with assessments ranging from 1 (Almost never) to 10 (Almost always). We also asked them a separate question about the extent to which they agreed or disagreed with the statement *Overall, this person is an effective leader* (1 = Strongly disagree and 5 = Strongly agree). The analysis showed that the effectiveness ratings of leaders by their direct reports increased systematically ($p < 0.001$) as leaders were observed engaging more and more frequently in the behaviors associated with encouraging the heart. There was a nearly 63 percent bump in effectiveness from the bottom to the top quartile.

FOCUS ON CLEAR STANDARDS

Imagine the frustration of Alice in *Alice in Wonderland* when she played a croquet match in which the mallets were flamingos, the wickets were playing-card soldiers, and the balls were hedgehogs. Everyone kept moving and the rules kept changing. There was no way to know how to play the game much less win it.

You needn't go down the rabbit hole to know how Alice felt. Haven't you, at one time or another, been at a place where you're not sure where you're supposed to be going, what the ground rules are that govern how to behave, or how you're doing along the way? And just when you think you've got the hang of it, the organization comes along and changes everything. This is a recipe for maddening frustration and pitiful performance. The antidote is making sure that people know both what they are supposed to do and how they are to do it. The data shows that people are proud to tell others about the organization they work for in direct relationship to the extent that their leaders "make it a point to let people know about his/her confidence in their abilities" (see figure 6.1).

If you want the people in your department to have a strong desire to succeed and make a difference, they must feel "in the flow." *Flow* occasions are those times when people experience pure enjoyment and effortlessness in what they do.[2] This psychological state requires clear standards—in both values and goals—because these help people concentrate their efforts and avoid distractions.

Is it better that people set their own goals, or should leaders set the goals for others? In the best of all worlds, individuals would set their own. Realistically, however, goals are often handed down, and the challenge is to find a middle ground—a path to determine mutually

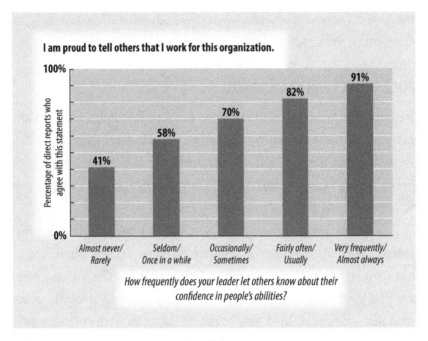

I am proud to tell others that I work for this organization.

Figure 6.1 The extent that leaders let others know about the confidence they have in people's abilities increases direct reports' pride.

acceptable objectives. People feel best about themselves and what they do when they have had the chance to influence some significant amount of their work responsibilities. Your challenge—and opportunity—is to make sure that people know the end they are serving and that what they are doing is important. With this in mind, they have a context for why they should both care and be willing to exert discretionary efforts to make a difference.

Without standards and goals, tasks in organizations often feel like just busywork. Clear standards and goals give work a context, something that individuals believe they can work on together and be recognized for accomplishing. They help people keep their eyes on the target, motivating them to put the phone in do-not-disturb mode, shut out the noise, and focus their time and efforts. Without goals, people won't know what to do with their own capabilities, as expressed in the old refrain *If you don't know where you are going, any road will get you there.*

Standards and goals, however, are not entirely sufficient. People also need to know if they're making progress toward a goal or just marking time. People's motivation to increase their productivity on a task goes up *only* when they have a challenging goal *and* receive feedback on their progress.[3] Goals without feedback, and feedback without goals, have little effect on motivation; however, together they keep people on track. The equivalent in academic advising would be working with a student who doesn't care about improving his performance (grades) or in the classroom with an instructor who does not provide her students with feedback on their assignments.

With clear goals and detailed feedback, people can become self-correcting, as well as more easily understand their place in the bigger picture. With feedback they can determine whether they are on the right track going forward and what help they need to be most productive. Many staff and faculty leaders echoed to us the sentiment that *You might not always like the feedback, but being aware of your shortcomings is essential for improving.* From a credibility perspective, how can you know if you are doing what you say you will do if you never get any feedback about your behavior? Feedback offers you a perspective about yourself and how you are doing that only others can provide. It's the avenue for understanding whether you are properly executing and advancing on your goal.

In one study of the effects of feedback on self-confidence, graduate students were praised, criticized, or received no feedback on their performance in a simulation of creative problem-solving. They had been told that their efforts would be compared with how well hundreds of others had done on the same task. Those who heard nothing about how well they did suffered as great a blow to their self-confidence as those who were criticized.[4] People hunger for feedback. They prefer to know how they are doing. No news has the same impact as bad news.

This is one of the reasons why efforts to abolish grades in schools and colleges almost always fail.

Expect the Best

Exemplary leaders have high expectations, both of themselves and of the people they work with. These expectations are powerful because they are the frames into which people fit reality. People are much more likely to see what they expect to see, even when their perspectives differ from what may actually be occurring. There is ample research evidence that people act in ways that are consistent with the expectations that other people have of them. If you expect others to fail, they probably will. If you expect them to succeed, they probably will.[5] The expectations you hold as a leader are the frame into which people fit their own realities.

Your expectations shape how you behave toward others. The high expectations that leaders have of others are based in large part on their expectations of themselves. This is one reason why it is so critical for leaders to Model the Way. Your own record of achievement and dedication, and your daily demonstrations of what and how things need to be accomplished, give credibility to the expectations you have of others.

Exemplary leaders treat people in a way that bolsters their self-confidence, making it possible for them to achieve more than they may have initially believed possible of themselves. Feeling appreciated by others increases a person's sense of self-worth, which in turn precipitates success at work and at home. Research and everyday experience confirm that men and women with high self-esteem "feel unique, competent, secure, empowered, and connected to the people around them."[6] This is true across all ages, levels of education, and socioeconomic backgrounds. If you have someone in your life who believes in you, and who continually reinforces that belief through their interactions with you, you are strongly influenced by that support.

Believing in others is an extraordinarily powerful force in propelling performance. If you want the people you work with to have a winning attitude, you must believe that they are already winners. It's not that they will be winners someday; they are winners right now! If you believe that people are winners, you will treat them that way. Moreover, if you want people to *be* winners, you have to behave in ways that communicate to them that they *are* winners. And it's not just about your words. It's also about your tone of voice, posture, gestures, and facial expressions. No yelling, frowning, cajoling, making fun of, or putting them down in front of others. Instead it's about being friendly, positive, supportive, and encouraging. Offer positive reinforcement, share lots of information, listen carefully to people's input, provide sufficient resources to do their jobs, give increasingly challenging assignments, and lend them your support and assistance.

It's a virtuous circle: you believe in your constituents' abilities, your favorable expectations cause you to be more positive in your actions, and those encouraging behaviors produce better results, reinforcing your belief that people can do it. And what's really powerful about this virtuous circle is that as people see that they are capable of extraordinary performance, they develop that expectation of themselves, and another virtuous circle begins.

If the potential exists within someone, you have to find a way to create the conditions that allow that individual to tap it. The emerging field of positive organizational psychology provides solid evidence of this. For example, leaders who foster an affirmative orientation in organizations, encourage virtuousness among people, and focus on achieving outcomes beyond the norm achieve significantly better results with their staffs.[7] There's growing proof that it pays to expect the best and to be positive.

Consider how two managers reacted when an athletic director proposed a new initiative in her division: "To my question 'Do you think this is a good idea?'" the athletic director reported, "one told me quite briskly, 'I have no idea if it is a good idea or not.' End of the conversation, really. When I asked another supervisor this same question, her response was quite different. She said, 'I don't have enough information to say if this is a good idea or not. But I do know that one of our most talented people is sharing this idea with me and she's really excited about it, so why don't you tell me more?'" Clearly, leaders can find ways, often quite simple ones, to nurture and bring out the best in those around them.

Positive expectations evoke positive images in the mind, where positive futures for self and others are first constructed. According to researchers, "We see what our imaginative horizon allows us to see."[8] Unless you and others can see yourselves as being successful, it is tough to produce the behavior that leads to success. Positive images make you more effective, relieving symptoms of illness and enhancing achievement.

For example, people were randomly assigned to different groups and instructed in effective bowling methods. Following these lessons, the bowlers were video-recorded practicing. One group of bowlers saw recordings of only the positive things they did; the other group saw only the negative. Those who saw only their positive moves improved significantly more than any of the other bowlers and were the most interested in continuing with the sport into the future.[9]

Before you can lead, you must believe in others and you must believe in yourself. Consistent with a growing body of research on the importance of growth mind-sets, holding the belief that people can change—that they can develop new skills and abilities—works magic on both the constituents and the leader who holds this expectation. People with a growth mind-set believe that their traits—for example of intelligence, talent, and abilities—can be learned and developed with time and effort, while those adhering to a fixed mind-set believe that such traits are limited in quantity from birth and cannot be substantially changed.[10]

During challenging times, especially when experiencing setbacks, people with fixed mind-sets can be expected to shy away from activities that may imply an area of deficit. Appearing "not dumb" drives their actions and decisions. Alternatively, those with a growth mind-set experience life as a journey in which challenges and setbacks are viewed as chances to learn and improve. Our research has found that people with a fixed mind-set are not as inclined to Encourage the Heart because they don't have very high expectations of what people "could" be capable of accomplishing; they tend to be on the lookout for what's wrong or not working rather than what's right and working well.[11]

Pay Attention

Leaders are out and about. They don't spend all of their time in an office or behind their desk. They're attending presentations, joining meetings, touring the campus, canvassing the student union, dropping in on labs, making presentations at alumni association gatherings, holding roundtable discussions, speaking to community groups, and dropping by colleagues' offices to check in. Being mobile goes with the leader's territory.

This is not purposeless wandering. Leaders are out there for a reason. One of the central reasons to be out and about is to show that you care. One way of showing you care is to *pay attention* to people, to what they are doing and how they are feeling. You have to look past the organizational diagrams, job descriptions, and the formal role people play and see the person inside. If you are clear about the standards you're looking for, and if you believe and expect that people will perform like winners, you're going to notice lots of examples of people both doing things right and doing the right things.

Paying attention can't be from a distance—reading reports or hearing secondhand. People you work with want to know who you are, how you feel, and whether you really do care. They want to see you in living color. Because proximity is the single best predictor of whether two people will talk to one another, you have to get close to people if you're going to communicate and know what is going on with them. On your part, this means regularly walking the hallways, attending various campus events (social, athletic, theatrical, and so on), frequenting the relevant places to hang out informally with others (like the staff lounge, faculty club, student union, and such), and even hitting the road for frequent visits with counterparts on other campuses and in other institutions.

Another benefit of getting out and about is that it increases your own visibility, making you better known to others. Don't take these actions just to be seen, however; do them because while you're getting to know other people, they're getting to know you. Paying attention and actively appreciating others increases their trust in you. And people trust more those they know over those who are strangers to them. With a norm of reciprocity, if people know you genuinely care about them, they're more likely to care about you.

Develop Friendships

Managerial myth says you shouldn't get too close to your colleagues, that you can't be friends with people at work. Well, set that myth aside. Over five years researchers observed groups of friends and groups of acquaintances (people who knew each other only slightly) performing motor-skill and decision-making tasks. The results were unequivocal: The groups composed of friends completed, on average, more than three times as many projects as the groups consisting merely of acquaintances. Regarding decision-making assignments, groups of friends were more than 20 percent more effective than groups of acquaintances.[17]

There is an important caveat, however: friends have to be firmly committed to the group's goals. If not, friends may not do better than anyone else. This is precisely why it is necessary that you are clear about standards and create conditions of shared vision and values. When it comes to performance, commitment to standards and good relations between people go together.

People are more willing to follow someone they like and trust. Becoming fully trusted, as previously noted, requires that you ante up first by being open yourself: open to others and open *with* others. Just as an open door is a physical demonstration of a willingness to let others in, an open heart is an emotional demonstration. This means letting others know more about you—what you care about, why you make the choices you do, and so forth. We don't mean tabloid-style disclosures. We mean talking about your hopes and dreams, your family and friends, your interests and pursuits—the same things you'd like to know about them.

When you're open, you make yourself vulnerable; this vulnerability is what makes you more human and more trustworthy to others. If neither person in a relationship takes the risk of trusting, at least a little, the relationship remains stalled at a low level of caution and suspicion; there's no connection. If leaders want the higher levels of performance that come with trust and collaboration, they must demonstrate their trust *in* others before asking for trust *from* others.

This is something that Cathy Avila understood and put into practice as a residential learning community director. "As a leader," Cathy told us, "I am an open book. I share very personal pieces of myself so that the people I lead have a thorough picture of my journey through life up until that point and will better understand how I work and why I work the way I do." Cathy soon discovered that when she demonstrated her trust in the residence staff by being the first to share personal information, challenges, goals, and fears, it made a big difference. For some staff, "it was the first time an adult (let alone their boss) had been honest and up-front with them." By opening her heart, Cathy motivated staff members to share their deeper selves with others in the group.

Disclosing information can be risky. You can't be sure that other people will appreciate your candor, empathize with your experiences, agree with your aspirations, buy in to your plans, or interpret your words and actions in the way you intend. But in demonstrating the willingness to take such risks, as Cathy did, you encourage others to take a similar risk—and thereby the first necessary steps to find common ground for building mutual trust.

Personalize Recognition

A familiar complaint about recognition is that it's too often highly predictable and impersonal. A one-size-fits-all approach to recognition feels disingenuous, forced, and thoughtless. It's like how birthday celebrations are done at restaurants: the staff sings to someone, and people at other tables start singing even though they don't know the person. No matter how well intended, over time these routines can increase cynicism and actually damage credibility. You have to do more than provide drive-by praise, simply walking around the campus, saying, "Thank you, whoever you are, whatever you are doing." It is essential to pay attention to the likes and dislikes of each person on your team. To make recognition meaningful, you have to get to know your constituents. By personalizing recognition, you send the message that you took the time to notice the achievement, sought out the responsible individual, and delivered the appreciation in a timely manner.

When Karyn Bechtel was transforming what she called a "'bunch of fellowships' into a 'fellowship program,'" she made it a point to make personal connections between people's contributions to the selection process and the outcomes of their selections. Karyn didn't just write thank-you notes; she personalized each one. She also shared with them "lists of selected Fellows and showed how particular application materials and their specific recommendations were critical in the decision process." This personalization and public acknowledgment was a boost for everyone involved. She also provided recognition when she asked someone to explain how he pulled off an extraordinary achievement. Showing interest in the story behind the accomplishment honors both the results as well as the person who reached them.[13]

Recognition that is not personalized will quickly be forgotten and discounted. When we've asked people to tell us about their *most meaningful recognitions,* they consistently report that they are "personal." They say that it feels special. "A sincere word of thanks from the right person at the right time," other researchers note, "can mean more to an employee than a raise, a formal award, or a whole wall of certificates and plaques."[14]

The extent to which recognition and rewards are applied to each individual in a personal (rather than an impersonal) manner also explains a lot about how leaders and their organizations get a motivational bang for their buck (or not) from recognizing people's contributions. Leaders bring out the best in others not by building fires *under* people but by igniting fires *within* them. Acknowledging people's accomplishments makes them feel valued and trusted, reinforces that progress is being made, and inspires that individual, and others, to even greater effort and levels of performance.

What personalized recognition comes down to is *thoughtfulness.* You need to be authentic and sincerely care about the person. Take those observations you've made about an individual and ask, *What would really make this special and unique for her? What could I do to make this a memorable experience so that he always remembers how important his contributions are?*

Use a Creative Mix of Recognitions and Rewards

Don't make the mistake of assuming that individuals respond only to monetary rewards. Although salary increases and bonuses are certainly valued, individual needs for and appreciation of rewards and recognition extend much further. And, by the way, studies reveal that most people will use a cash bonus to pay bills, and after a few months they won't even remember how they spent the money or even how much they had received.[15] The bigger problem with cash, and even raises, is that their supply is limited, especially in higher education, and most often they are not within your direct or timely control.

People respond to all kinds of informal acknowledgments. Verbal recognition of performance in front of one's peers and visible reminders, such as certificates, plaques, trophies, and mementos, are also powerful commemorations of achievements. For example, after one faculty member received a prestigious writing award for the third time, his department chair presented him with a beat-up hat because winning the award was "old hat" for this person.

There are lots of other ways to show appreciation that are within your scope of influence and ability. For example, you can send a handwritten note (even better than an electronic message), make a comment in a meeting about someone's good work or achievement, or just stop by their cubicle or office to let them know that you are aware of the great work they are doing. Spontaneous and unexpected rewards, people have told us, are typically more meaningful than the expected formal rewards. And to make it the most effective, be sure that your recognition is highly specific and given in close proximity to the appropriate behavior. Being too general or too late diminishes the positive power of the gesture.

One of the most important benefits of being out and about as a leader is that you can personally observe people doing things right and then recognize and reward them either on the spot or at the next public opportunity. Besides, relying on an organization's formal reward system typically requires considerably greater effort than making use of *intrinsic* rewards—those that are built in to the work itself, including such factors as a sense of accomplishment, a chance to be creative, the challenge of the work, and the satisfaction of a job well done. Despite what some might think, studies reveal that intrinsic rewards are far more important than salary and fringe benefits in improving job satisfaction, commitment, retention, and performance.[16]

Often it's the simple, personal gestures that are the most meaningful rewards. Personal congratulations rank at the top of the most powerful nonfinancial motivators identified by employees.[17] Surveys also indicate that 79 percent of employees who quit their jobs cite a lack of appreciation as a key reason.[18] Lisa Millora, senior assistant provost, for example, talks about how important it is to appreciate others, even if it is a simple thank-you for their time, effort, trust, and willingness to come into a conversation. She never takes for granted the amount of work that any of the provost office's administrative staff do, and she always sends them handwritten thank-you notes. She also always tries to circle back when people send her feedback on an issue, even, she says, "if I'm not going to do anything with it; I want to let them know that I really appreciate their input." Unlike Lisa, not enough people make sufficient use of that powerful but inexpensive two-word reward: "thank you."

Jane Binger, responsible for leadership development and education at a medical school, routinely checks in with people about how they would like to be recognized. She has found that most just want a simple gesture acknowledging that their work was appreciated and valued. Ron Siers, as a department chair, told us that he finds it "extremely powerful" to provide time at the beginning of each faculty meeting for people to acknowledge the contributions and efforts of their colleagues. "No one wants to be taken for granted or feel unappreciated," he says; "moreover, doing this strongly correlates our appreciations with our core values."

There are few, if any, more basic needs than being noticed, recognized, and appreciated for your efforts. That's for everyone on campus—academics, engineers, artists, counselors, residence advisers, budget analysts, athletic coaches, facilities staff, and those in the president's office. Institutions with the greatest volume of appreciation tend to be the most innovative and vibrant organizations.

FOSTER A SPIRIT OF COMMUNITY

All over the world, in every country, in every culture, and on every campus, people stop working on certain days or occasions during the year and take the time to celebrate. Impromptu ceremonies are often convened to rejoice in the acceptance of a colleague's manuscript for publication, the award of a new contract for a research laboratory, the opening of a new facility or art installation, reaccreditation, and the like. Banquets are organized to acknowledge individuals and groups who've accomplished the extraordinary. Colleagues get together with one another at the end of work on an exhausting task force or promotion committee and give each other high-fives for a job well done. Even in tragic times, people come together in remembrance and song to honor those before them and to reaffirm their common humanity.

Why do people take time away from work to gather together, tell stories, and raise their spirits? Sure, everyone needs a break from the pace and intensity of their job, but celebrating is not a frivolous excuse to goof off. Celebrations are among the most significant ways people have to proclaim their respect and gratitude, to renew their sense of community, and to remind themselves of their binding values and traditions. Celebrations serve as important a purpose in the long-term health of campus institutions as does the daily performance of tasks.

What leaders know from practice is confirmed in our research. Performance improves when leaders bring people together to rejoice in their achievements and to reinforce their shared principles. By bringing people together, sharing the lessons from success, and getting personally involved, leaders strengthen in others the courage required to make a difference and make extraordinary things happen in their organizations.

Individual recognition increases the recipient's sense of worth, and it improves performance. Public celebrations have this effect *and more*. Every time you can bring the group together is a chance to renew commitment. Exemplary leaders seldom let pass any opportunity to make sure that everyone knows why they're all there and how they're going to act in service of that purpose. Whether it's in honor of an individual, group, or organizational achievement, celebrations offer leaders the perfect opening to explicitly communicate and reinforce the actions and behaviors that are important in realizing shared values and goals.

Celebrations are much more than parties; they're ceremonies and rituals that create meaning. At such occasions it's vitally important to be clear about the statements you're making and the behaviors you're reinforcing. You should be fully aware that people are going to leave the event remembering and repeating what you say and what they see. You should always be personally prepared with the key messages you want to send. Each time ask yourself, *What values do we hold dear, what visions do we aspire to realize, and what behaviors do we want to reinforce?* Be prepared for every public opportunity to reinforce the culture and the meaning you want to instill.

Provide Social Support

Supportive relationships at work—relationships characterized by a genuine belief in and advocacy for the interests of others—are critically important to maintaining personal and organizational vitality. Ceremonies and celebrations are opportunities to build healthier groups and to enable members of the organization to get to know and care about one another.

"Life is too short to be miserable," says Charles Ambelang, vice president for human resources (although he came to the university originally as director of the student union). "You want to have a work experience that allows you to engage with others, share a laugh, see the humor in a situation, and thank people for doing a good job." Unofficially, Charlie is referred to as HR's CEO—chief encouragement officer.

When he took the helm, the HR workgroup was demoralized and fearful. The team was used to an environment in which there was little recognition of success and severe consequences for failure. His staff told us, "The HR team needed someone to appreciate our individual and collective efforts. Charlie focused on encouraging everyone to be a contributing member of the team and to work toward a collective commitment to deeply held values and service to the campus community."

Charlie regularly encourages members of the department by letting them know that he believes in them and has confidence that they will be successful. He also does crazy, spur-of-the-moment things to celebrate the team's accomplishments, like going to the grocery store and buying boxes of popsicles and ice cream bars. He'll return to the office with his booty of icy goodness, empty the mail cart, load it up with treats, and then play ice-cream truck music on his smartphone while cruising through the office, giving everyone their pick of frozen delight.

Charlie sets up celebratory outings for the team, such as an "HR at the movies" night. When a recent blockbuster was released, he bought 40 tickets so that each HR staff member could ask a family member or friend to join them for the film and then dinner afterward to discuss what they saw and how it translated back to their work. He organizes a Friday-night trip to the local Minor League Baseball game for HR staff and their families. "It's a fun and relaxing way to end the week and spend time getting to know more about our fellow team members as well as their families," one of his staff members explained.

Charlie's actions and the experience of the HR department confirm our research. Performance improves when leaders provide social support by publicly honoring those who have excelled and been an example to others. It also goes up when leaders demonstrate that *We are all in this together* and when they make the work environment a place where people want to be, stay, and work hard. An extensive 10-year study revealed that social support networks are essential for sustaining the motivation to serve. Service-performance shortfalls in organizations are highly correlated with the absence of social support and teamwork.[19] Coworkers who support one another and achieve together can be an antidote to service burnout. Working with others should be rejuvenating, inspirational, and fun.

Researchers have found that social support—more specifically, having friends at work—is good for your health, as well as for productivity. Those who report that they have a "best friend at work" are significantly more engaged, get more done in less time, have a safer workplace with fewer accidents, share ideas, feel informed, are innovative, and indicate having more fun on the job.[20] Conversely, there are few things more painful than being shunned at work.

Strong human connections produce spectacular results when leaders and constituents alike get personally involved with the task and with their colleagues. When people feel a strong sense of affiliation and attachment to the people they work with, they are much more likely to have a higher sense of personal well-being, to feel more committed to the organization, and to perform at higher levels. When people feel distant and detached, they're unlikely to get much of anything significant done at all.

One of the things that make people most miserable is being alone. Celebrations remind people that they aren't alone in their efforts and that they both need and can count on one another to make things happen and be successful. These reminders build the courage to continue in times of turmoil and stress and reinforce the fact that it takes a group of people working together with a common purpose, in an atmosphere of trust and collaboration, to achieve beyond the ordinary.

The case for social support is further boosted by the fact that information exchange is more likely to be facilitated, whether in formal or informal interactions, when people like one another. Even in the age of the internet and smartphones, people are just more likely to share things when they're in a gathering with other people than when they're sitting alone at their workstations. When celebrations cut across functional and hierarchical boundaries, people get a chance to exchange ideas with and be stimulated by people outside their own areas.

Be Personally Involved

Wherever you find a strong culture built around shared values, you'll also find endless examples of leaders who personally live those values. Leaders make their values tangible by putting them into action. The resident adviser who chooses the less desirable suite because it's closer to the central hub of the building, the faculty member who works all weekend to get papers returned to students on time, and the academic administrator who continues to teach classes to stay in touch with students—they all show others that living the values is important. It's the same with Encourage the Heart: whether through individual recognition or group celebration, the leader has to set the example.

The only way to show people that you genuinely care and that you appreciate their efforts is to be out there with them, personally involved. You've got to walk the corridors, stroll around the residence halls, eat in the cafeteria, wander through the library, solicit and listen to feedback, and tell stories about accomplishments. Such visibility may make you vulnerable, but most assuredly it makes you more real and more genuine. To your colleagues, you're not just the graduate programs director but that person who talked with them at the open house. You're not only the director of public safety but the person who came to the athletic department offices to brainstorm about making players and guests from visiting teams feel more welcomed. Authenticity goes up when you get personally involved. By directly and visibly showing others that you care, that you want them to be successful, that you'll cheer them along, you're sending a positive signal. Moreover, you're more likely to see others take these same actions if

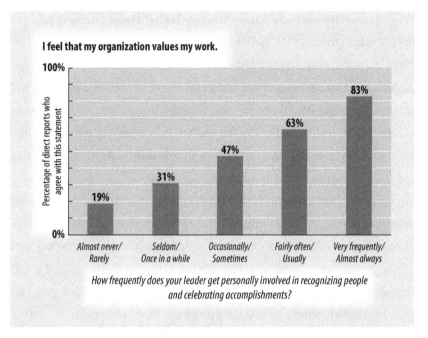

I feel that my organization values my work.

Figure 6.2 The extent that leaders get personally involved in recognizing people and celebrating accomplishments increases people's feeling that their work is valued.

you do them. It's that simple. Those people who most strongly feel that their organizations value their work are also those who most agree that their leaders "get personally involved in recognizing people and celebrating accomplishments," as shown in figure 6.2.

Another benefit of being out and about, and getting personally involved in showing you care, is that this experience provides you with an opportunity to find and tell stories that put a human face on values. First-person examples are always more powerful and memorable than third-party examples. It's that striking difference between *I saw for myself* and *Someone told me about*. You should constantly be on the lookout for "catching people doing things right" in your department, and this can't be done by staying behind a desk, counter, or computer screen.

You need to see and know firsthand what's being done right, not only so that you can let individuals and teams know to keep up the good work but also so that you can tell others about their actions that make a difference. As a result, you can share up-close-and-personal accounts of what it actually means in a real-time context to put shared values into practice. You make the values more than pronouncements; you make them come alive. You champion role models in your department or institution whom everyone can relate to.

Telling stories about how people on campus demonstrated their commitment to values is one of the quickest and most effective ways of translating information about how people are supposed to act and make decisions.[21] Through storytelling you can better accomplish the objectives of teaching, mobilizing, and motivating than you can through bullet points in a slide presentation or tweets on a mobile device. Listening to and understanding the stories that leaders tell informs people more about the values and culture of an organization than company policies or the employee manual. The stories communicate what really goes on in the organization. Well-told stories reach inside people and pull them along. They simulate the actual experience of being there and give people an emotionally compelling way to learn what is really important about the experience. Reinforcing the stories through celebrations deepens the connections.

Because leadership is a relationship, people are much more likely to enlist in initiatives led by those with whom they feel a personal affiliation. It's the human connection between leaders and constituents that ensures more commitment and more support. Lisa, on behalf of herself and the entire provost office, makes every effort to ensure that faculty members know that what they do has an impact that is recognized campuswide. Creating a spirit of community to celebrate victories and hosting celebrations from time to time has characterized her entire career. With student groups, she always puts in the effort to gather them around and distribute certificates or small tokens of appreciation. With faculty and staff, she arranges lunches and dinners to express gratitude for people's time and efforts. According to Lisa, none of these has to be a grand event; "really it's a spirit of gathering." Finding a way to say thank you—and genuinely meaning it—is a very concrete way of showing respect and enhancing personal credibility.

We started the discussion of The Five Practices of Exemplary Leadership with Model the Way, and here we are again. If you want others to believe in something and behave according to those beliefs, you have to be personally involved and set the example. You have to practice what you preach. If you want people to stay true to shared values, you have to stay true to them, as well. If you want to build and maintain a culture of excellence and distinction, you have to recognize, reward, reinforce, and celebrate exceptional efforts and successes. You must get personally involved in celebrating the actions that contribute to and sustain the culture. And, if you want people to have the courage to continue the quest in the face of great adversity, you have to encourage them yourself.

QUESTIONS FOR REFLECTION: *ENCOURAGE THE HEART*

Leaders expect to do their best and expect the best of their constituents. With clear standards they help people focus on what needs to be done. By paying attention, offering encouragement, personalizing appreciation, and maintaining a positive outlook, leaders stimulate, rekindle, and focus people's energies and drive.

You need to recognize individual contributions to vision and values and be creative in demonstrating appreciation. Celebrating values and victories together reinforces the fact that extraordinary performance is the result of many people's efforts. By celebrating people's accomplishments visibly, and in group settings, you nourish and sustain a team spirit. Telling stories about individuals who have made exceptional efforts and achieved phenomenal successes provides role models for others to emulate. Social interaction increases people's commitments to the standards of the group and has a profound effect on people's well-being. By getting personally involved in recognition and celebrations, you set the example and foster a culture of support and community.

In developing your competence in the leadership practice of Encourage the Heart, spend some time reflecting on the following questions. After you've given them sufficient consideration, let others know what you are thinking and willing to do.

▶ How can you be even more conscientious and thoughtful about saying "thank you" to people who are making a difference, even if the outcome is part of their job description?

▶ In recognizing both individual and group accomplishments, how can you more directly link the results achieved to shared values and purpose?

▶ In what creative ways can you get people together to celebrate the accomplishments of the unit, marking the progress that's been made?

▶ How can you best remind people that achievements are the result of the entire group's efforts and not just the work of a single individual? What creative strategies can you develop for ensuring that people feel they are "all for one and one for all"?

Leadership Is Everyone's Business

BEYOND THE LEADERSHIP PRACTICES, and beyond the essential behaviors, actions, and reflections, there is another fundamental truth about leadership that you should appreciate: *leadership is everyone's business*. This is as true in institutions of higher learning as it is in manufacturing, high technology, health care, government, military services, and nonprofit agencies. Regardless of organization, function, discipline, or over time and geography, the best leaders understand this reality. No one is at his or her personal best as a leader without involving others in making the extraordinary happen.

While serving as dean, John Seybolt came to have a clear view of his school's future. He knew that given the extremely high competition for outstanding faculty, the school needed major new sources of external funding. As he told us, "My fondest dream at the time was that we would receive a significant endowment for the school, giving it the freedom and flexibility to fund people and projects that could really make a difference. I also dreamed that because of these gifts, people would 'stand up and take notice' of the school and its potential." The school had long been referred to as "a hidden treasure." John countered that statement by pointing out that "a hidden treasure is just that—*hidden*—and that's not what we want to be."

John talked a lot about what private funding sources could mean at a state institution. He spread the feeling that *This is an exciting time* and *What I can do here will make a difference.* He challenged the status quo by asking people to do some things they had never done before. He urged faculty members to speak with local community and corporate leaders about the importance of their research, and he asked community leaders to work with the school in new ways. Similarly, he involved faculty, students, and alumni in imagining the future possibilities that an endowment could enable for the school.

Ultimately, the school received a multimillion-dollar endowment from a single individual, earmarked to "build and sustain the intellectual infrastructure" of the school. At the time this was the largest single gift in the history of the state and among the 10 largest single gifts ever to a US school.

When asked if he and his group received any special recognition for their efforts, John's answer was telling: "We received the greatest reward possible: a financial security blanket designed to help ensure that the school would be able to continue to attract and retain prominent faculty members and outstanding students and provide seed funding for innovative programs that would enable it to thrive." John described the "reward" in terms of the benefits to the school at large and not to himself or even to any one group of constituents. He put *we* first.

This achievement wasn't easy. The school had never focused much attention on significant fundraising; it was, after all, part of a state (public) university. Yet John was driven in his quest, and he was not alone. He involved and mobilized others on campus and off; he modeled, inspired, challenged, enabled, and encouraged—all along the way.

Like John, many of the people we studied became exemplary leaders because they passionately believed they could make something significantly better than it was or had been. They saw an opportunity where others didn't; they seized on a possibility where others had been discouraged by the probabilities. They mobilized others on behalf of a cause and shared the necessary resources so that others could become leaders in their own right. Not every leader initiated the personal-best leadership projects that they wrote and talked about, yet each rose to the occasion. Many accepted an assignment and then found something within themselves that they hadn't known they had. No one knows their true strength until challenged to bring it forth. Admissions Counselor Paulo Garcia offered this reflection from her Personal-Best Leadership Experience: "I must admit I was apprehensive to take on the role because I had not seen myself as a natural leader. However, upon taking up the challenge, I realized I could be a leader."

LEADERSHIP IS LEARNED

There persists a pernicious myth that leadership is reserved for only a handful of special people. That myth is perpetuated every time someone asks, "Are leaders born or made?" Whenever people ask us this question—which is almost every time we give a speech or conduct a class or workshop—our answer, always offered with a smile, is this: "We've never met a leader who was not born. *All* leaders are born. So are all college presidents, deans, coaches, teachers, scholars, registrars, directors, actors, accountants, artists, parents—you name it." We're all born with various sets of skills and abilities. What you do with what you have before you die, well, that's entirely up to you.

There's another leadership myth that stands in the way of personal and organizational success—that leadership is associated with position. It's an assumption that leadership starts with a capital *L* and that when you're on top you're automatically a leader. This view is part of a larger hero myth that inhibits people from seizing the initiative and keeps them waiting for someone to ride in and save the day.[1]

It's pure mythology that only a lucky few can ever understand the intricacies of leadership. Leadership is not a place, it's not a gene, and it's not a secret code. The truth is that leadership is an observable set of skills and abilities that are useful whether one is in the chancellor's office, bookstore, library, classroom, dining hall, housing, human resources, public safety, information technology, media service, or student development. Any skill can be strengthened, honed, and enhanced—given the motivation and desire—through practice and feedback, along with good role models and coaching. So, all leaders are born *and* all leaders are made.

It's very curious and revealing that no one has ever asked us, "Can *management* be taught? Are *managers* born or made?" Why is management viewed as a set of skills and abilities while leadership is typically seen as a set of innate personality characteristics? It's simple. People *assume* that management can be taught, and because they do, hundreds of business schools have been established, and each year thousands of management courses are taught. By assuming that people can learn the attitudes, skills, and knowledge associated with good management practices, schools and universities have raised the caliber of managers. They've also contributed to the idea that good management skills are attainable.

The same can be said for leadership. It's not the absence of leadership potential that inhibits the development of more leaders; it's the persistence of the myth that leadership can't be taught and can't be learned. This debilitating myth is a far more powerful deterrent to leadership development than are the talents of any person or the fundamentals of the leadership process. And this myth is entirely antithetical to the essence of any educational philosophy.

Leadership *can* be taught, but not solely in classrooms, seminars, or books such as this one. Not only do you need a conceptual foundation but, more importantly, you also have to have guidance, practice, feedback, and reinforcement. You can't read a book on public speaking and suddenly expect to be more comfortable and a better speaker in front of groups. You wouldn't accept a physician who has only academic knowledge. Leadership in this regard is a clinical skill and is learned, developed, and honed in practice settings.

Our collective task is to liberate the leader within each and every person. Rather than view leadership as an innate set of character traits—a self-fulfilling prophecy that dooms each campus and society at large to have only a few good leaders—it's far healthier and more productive to assume that it's possible for *everyone* to learn to lead. By assuming that leadership is learnable, you can discover how many good leaders there really are. Somewhere, sometime, the leader within each individual may get the call to step forward—for the department, the function, the program, and the college, as well as for their families, congregations, neighborhoods, and communities. By believing in yourself and your capacity to learn to lead, you make sure you'll be prepared when that call comes.

Surely you shouldn't mislead people into believing that they can attain unrealistic goals, but neither should you assume that only a few can ever achieve excellence in leadership—or in any other human endeavor. Those who are most successful at bringing out the best in others are those who set achievable "stretch" goals and believe that they can develop the talents of others.

The most effective leaders are continuously learning. They see *all* experiences as learning experiences, not just those sessions in a formal classroom or workshop. They're always looking for ways to improve themselves and their organizations. By reading this book, reflecting on the questions at the end of each chapter, and engaging in other personal development activities, you're demonstrating a predisposition to lead. Even if some people think that they're not able to learn to lead, you must believe that you can. That's where it all starts—with your own belief in yourself.

Regardless of how much you now know about leadership, becoming the best leader you can be is a lifelong journey of continuous improvement. And in keeping with the scientific method embedded in the scholarly traditions of higher education, this requires hypothesis testing. It means persistent experimentation, reflection, drawing lessons from experience and applying them to subsequent experiments, receiving new feedback, analyzing the outcomes, and so on in a continuous iterative process. In doing so you become a leadership *researcher,* offering proof to the claim that the best leaders are the best learners.[2]

CONTRASTS AND CONTRADICTIONS

In analyzing thousands of case studies, numerous interviews, and millions of survey responses, we identified The Five Practices of Exemplary Leadership as an operating system for leaders. We learned that in performing at their personal bests, people Model the Way, Inspire a Shared Vision, Challenge the Process, Enable Others to Act, and Encourage the Heart. Along with many scholars, we have found that leaders who more frequently engage in The Five Practices are significantly more likely to achieve extraordinary results than those who use these practices less often.

That said, here is a warning: Any leadership practice *can* become destructive. Virtues can become vices. There's a point at which each of The Five Practices, taken to extremes, can lead you astray. Finding your voice and setting an example are essential to establishing your credibility and making a difference—but an obsession with being seen as a role model can lead to being too focused on your own values and ways of doing things. It can cause you to discount others' views and be closed to feedback. It can push you into isolation for fear of losing privacy or being "found out." It can also blind you to being more concerned with style than substance.

Leaders set themselves apart from other credible people by being forward-looking and communicating a clear and shared vision of the future. Yet a singular focus on one vision of the future can keep you from seeing or even imagining other possibilities as well as prevent you from acknowledging the realities of the present. It can cause you to miss the exciting prospects that are just out of your sight or make you hang on just a little too long to an old, tired, out-of-date technology. Exploiting your powers of inspiration can cause others to surrender their will because your own energy, enthusiasm, and charm may be so magnetic that others don't think for themselves.

Challenging the process is essential to promoting innovation and progressive change. Seizing the initiative and taking risks are necessary for learning and continuous improvement; but taken to extremes, you can cause needless turmoil, confusion, and paranoia. If you seldom slow down enough to give people the opportunity to gain confidence and competence, they'll lose their motivation to try new things. Change for change's sake can be just as demoralizing as complacency.

Collaboration and teamwork are essential to getting extraordinary things done in today's turbulent world. Innovation depends on high degrees of trust. People must be given the power to control their own lives if they are to accomplish great things. But an overreliance on collaboration and trust may be rooted in the avoidance of conflict or an unwillingness to examine decisions critically. These dynamics may be a way of evading accountability or *not* taking charge when the situation requires. Delegating power and responsibility can become a way of dumping too much on others when they're not adequately prepared to handle it.

People do perform at higher levels when they are challenged and encouraged. Personal recognition and group celebration inspire the spirit and momentum that can carry a group forward even during the toughest of challenges. At the same time, a constant focus on who should be recognized and when celebrations should be held can turn you into a gregarious minstrel. You can lose sight of the mission because you're having so much fun. Don't become overly consumed by all the perks and pleasures and lose sight of the purpose behind the recognition.

Far more insidious than all of these possible vices, however, is the treachery of hubris, the Achilles' heel of leadership. It's good to be royalty, gratifying to have influence, and exhilarating to have scores of people cheering your every word. In many all-too-subtle ways, it's easy to be seduced by power and importance. All evil leaders have been infected with the disease of hubris, becoming bloated with an exaggerated sense of self and pursuing their own sinister ends. How can you avoid this?

The answer is humility.[3] You can avoid excessive pride only if you recognize that you don't know everything, that there are other smart, talented, experienced, and dedicated people.[4] Knowing that you're only human helps—that you are never as good or as bad as others may believe. It also helps to recognize that nothing great was ever accomplished alone—that you need the help of others. In the context of education, it's only fitting to note that leaders are constantly learning. Listen to what your colleagues have to say. Find the honesty to admit your mistakes and the grace to step back, correct, and forgive yourself. Hold on to humility: it's the only way we know to resolve the conflicts and contradictions of leadership.

In fact, research on organizations that transition from mediocrity (or worse) to long-term superiority reveals a remarkable pattern of humility among the chief executives of "good-to-great" companies: "In contrast to the very *I*-centric style of the comparison leaders, we were struck by how the good-to-great leaders *didn't* talk about themselves.... They'd talk about the company and the contributions of other executives as long as we'd like but would deflect discussion about their own contributions."[5] Similarly, their compelling modesty is perhaps why many of the best leaders within higher education are not the ones to grab the headlines in *The Chronicle of Higher Education* and the local or national press or gain rock-star status in the popular leader-as-hero culture. Instead these leaders focus their attention and will on their institutions and on others.

This is consistent with our own findings. The leaders in higher education whom we've met and interviewed cared more about the institution than they did about their own successes. As we've discussed, exemplary leaders know that they can't do it alone and they act accordingly. They lack the pride and pretense displayed by many people who may have succeeded in the short term but leave behind a weak organization that fails to thrive after their departure. Instead, with self-effacing humor[6] and generous and sincere credit to others, they reach higher and higher levels of achievement; they make extraordinary things happen.

There is yet another way to avoid the temptations of power that lead to becoming overbearing and presumptuous. Refuse to become one-dimensional, focused narrowly on your work and organization. Do not allow work to consume you. Get involved in the world that surrounds you. The very best leaders have numerous pursuits and interests—arts, literature, science, technology, entertainment, sports, politics, law, religion, friends, and family.

There's one other valuable lesson that will help you deal with the contrasts and contradictions of leadership. Nothing in our research even hints that leaders should be perfect. Leaders aren't saints. They're human beings full of flaws and failings like everyone else. They make mistakes. We advise all aspiring leaders to adopt the attitude of a novice—to always remain open and full of wonder. The best leaders, as we've said, continue to be the best learners.

KEEP HOPE ALIVE

People look to willingly follow those leaders who demonstrate an enthusiastic and genuine belief in the capacity of others, who strengthen people's will, who supply the means to achieve, and who express optimism for the future. People want leaders who remain passionate and maintain a bit of humor (especially not taking themselves too seriously) despite obstacles and setbacks. Every college and university—and the business of higher education— desperately needs leaders with a positive, confident, can-do approach.

Being at one's personal best as a leader is never an easy or straightforward experience. Everyone we talked with acknowledged the hard work, disappointments, setbacks, mistakes, misgivings, and sacrifices they endured. They encountered them when reviewing and updating curriculum, revising the faculty handbook, establishing a new service-learning program, or moving from the concept of dormitories to residential learning communities. They were evident when building a new twenty-first-century library, holistically integrating student affairs programs with the academic affairs programs, requiring a common platform across the campus for information services and technology, bringing alumni and development programs under one roof, and determining a comprehensive marketing strategy for the campus.

Leaders in every situation and circumstance needed to keep hope alive, even in the most difficult times. They had to strengthen their constituents' belief that today's struggle would produce a more promising tomorrow. Leaders demonstrated their faith and confidence by holding themselves accountable, by not asking anyone else to do something they wouldn't be willing to do themselves, and by accepting responsibility for the quality of the lives of their constituents, colleagues, programs, departments, and even institutions. Even when everything goes wrong or when they suffer resounding defeats, leaders display an unwavering commitment to the cause.

I knew in my heart what we were trying to do, and why we were trying to do it, and what I was prepared to do myself to make it happen is a phrase heard over and over again by those who provide leadership in higher education. Jeanne Rosenberger didn't let go of her belief that students would live up to their responsibilities. Alan Glassman never stopped believing that his faculty colleagues across the campus could work collectively in the strategic-planning process with the central administration to rebuild and revitalize the university. Kent

Koth pioneered an alternative spring break program and didn't ask of his students anything he wasn't already doing or willing to do in service to others.

Without hope there can be no courage—and exercising leadership in college and university settings is no place for the timid. This is the time and place for optimism, imagination, and enthusiasm. Leaders must summon their will if they are to mobilize the personal and organizational resources to triumph against the odds. Hope is essential to achieving the highest levels of performance. Hope enables people to transcend the difficulty of today and envision the potential of tomorrow. Hope enables people to bounce back even after being stressed, stretched, and depressed. Hope enables people to find the will and the way to aspire to greatness.[7]

And yet hope is not the final thing that you must keep alive. We have one more lesson to share.

THE SECRET TO SUCCESS IN LIFE

Early in our study of leadership bests, we were fortunate to cross paths with US Army Major General John H. Stanford. During his service, John endured military tours in Vietnam, was highly decorated, headed up the army's Military Traffic Management Command (and handled the logistics for Desert Storm), and had the steadfast loyalty of his troops. Following his military career, he became the chief administrator for Fulton County, Georgia (which includes Atlanta), as it geared up to host the 1996 Summer Olympics. He was subsequently recruited to the position of superintendent for the Seattle, Washington, school district, where he sparked a revolution in public education.

John was a renaissance individual who served at the local, national, and international levels. His distinguished career transcended and bridged the armed services, public administration, and education. His answer to one of our interview questions significantly influenced our understanding of leadership at the deepest level, and he gave voice to how we saw him live his life.

We asked John how he would go about developing leaders, whether at a college or university, in the military, in government, in the nonprofit sector, or in private business. Here is what he told us:

> When anyone asks me that question, I tell them I have the secret to success in life. The secret to success is to stay in love. Staying in love gives you the fire to ignite other people, to see inside other people, to have a greater desire to get things done than other people. A person who is not in love doesn't really feel the kind of excitement that helps them to get ahead and to lead others and to achieve. I don't know any other fire, any other thing in life that is more exhilarating and is more positive a feeling than love is.

"Staying in love" isn't the answer we expected to get—at least not when we *began* studying leadership. But after nearly 40 years of being leaders, researching leadership, and developing leaders, we continue to be struck by how many people use the word *love* freely when talking about their own motivations to lead and in explaining why they endured the hardships, made the personal sacrifices, and accomplished what they did.

Of all the things that sustain a leader over time, love is the most lasting. It's hard to imagine leaders on any college campus getting up day after day and putting in the long hours and hard work it takes to make a difference without having their hearts in it. This may just be the best-kept secret of successful leaders: *If you love what you're doing, you will never have to work.*

So, stay in love with leading. Stay in love with your colleagues who do the work. Stay in love with the students, faculty, staff, and alumni who are transformed because of their time at your institution. Stay in love with the scholarship, ideas, programs, and applications that emerge through and because of what you and so many others contribute.

Leadership is *not* an affair of the head. Leadership is, after all, an affair of the heart.

TAKE THE NEXT STEP

At the end of each chapter, we asked you to reflect on a few questions. Now at the end of this book, we have one final question for you: *What are you actually going to do now to be an even better leader?*

From the examples of leaders in this book and from decades of research and experience, we know that everyone can lead. But make no mistake. Leadership is never easy. Reading about leadership is easy. Attending a leadership training program is easy. Actually applying what you learn is *not* easy. When we teach seminars on leadership, we finish by asking participants if they heard anything that was too complex, too esoteric to understand, or too difficult to grasp. The answer is always no. The leadership challenge is not in knowing the concepts; it's in putting them into practice. Then we ask: *What are you actually going to do now to be an even better leader?*

We believe that you know what you can do to be an even better leader than you are right now, but *doing* it is a different story. To really change and improve, you first must fall deeply in love with the idea of being an exemplary leader. Then and only then will you have the strength and resilience necessary to overcome your hesitation and deeply ingrained habits. Pain and discomfort are inevitable on the leadership journey, but so are joy and the thrill of accomplishment if you stick with it.

In this book we've given you dozens of things you can do to improve your leadership skills in The Five Practices. *What are you going to do?* We hope that when you look around and say, "Something needs to change" or "Something can be improved or can be better than it is right now," you'll also look in the mirror and see that you are the person who could make the difference.

There's a popular riddle about 12 frogs that goes like this: If 12 frogs are sitting on a log at the edge of a pond and five of those 12 frogs decide to jump into the pond, how many frogs remain on the log? What's your answer? Seven? Zero? Twelve? Five?

The correct answer is 12. Twelve frogs remain on the log. Why? The reason is that there is a huge difference between *deciding* to do something and actually *doing* it. Now that you've finished reading this book, please keep the imperative of this riddle in mind.

You've read about how leadership makes a difference, and you've learned about The Five Practices of Exemplary Leadership operating system. You've been presented with numerous examples and illustrations about the behaviors of people in higher education who make extraordinary things happen. You've been presented with many questions and issues to reflect on and offered many suggestions on leadership actions you can take right now.

Decide to do something different that will make you an even better leader. Then hop off the log and get into the water!

Appendix:
The Research Basis
for This Book

While *Leadership in Higher Education* is written as a practical guide to enhance and support the abilities of higher-education leaders at all levels, the principles and practices described are based solidly in research.

Our work on leadership has its origins in a research project we began in 1983. We wanted to know what leaders did when they operated at their "personal best" in leading others. These were experiences in which people set, in their own perception, their individual leadership standard of excellence. We started with an assumption that to discover best practices we didn't have to interview and survey star performers in excellent companies. Instead we assumed that by asking people at all levels and across a broad array of organizational settings to describe extraordinary experiences, we would find and identify patterns of success.

The original Personal-Best Leadership Experience survey consisted of 38 open-ended questions; here is a sampling:

- *Who initiated the project?*

- *How prepared were you for this experience?*

■ *What special techniques and strategies did you use to get other
   people involved in the project?*

■ *How would you describe the character or feel of the experience?*

■ *What did you learn about leadership from this experience?*

The survey generally required one to two hours to complete, and more
than 550 of these in-depth surveys were collected during the initial
phase of our research. A short, two-page form was also completed by
another group of 780 managers.

In addition to the written case studies, we conducted 42 in-depth
interviews, primarily with managers in middle- to senior-level organizational positions in a wide variety of both public and private-sector
companies from around the world. The interviews generally took 45 to
60 minutes. Since these initial studies, our ongoing research files now
include more than 5,000 personal-best cases (and over 10,000 cases
using the short form), and we've interviewed more than 500 people
around the globe, representing individuals from all types of organizations and from all levels and functions.

The *Leadership Practices Inventory* was created both to validate
the findings of our qualitative studies and to provide an assessment
measure to help people develop their leadership abilities. The items on
the LPI were derived by recording specific one-sentence descriptions
of behavior demonstrated in the Personal-Best Leadership Experiences. Statements were selected, modified, or discarded following
lengthy discussions and iterative feedback sessions with respondents
and subject-matter experts, as well as through empirical analyses of
the behavior-based statements.

The LPI contains 30 statements, six essential behaviors associated
with each of The Five Practices of Exemplary Leadership. Participating
individuals complete the LPI-Self and request five to 10 people familiar
with their behavior to complete the LPI-Observer. The LPI-Observer
is voluntary, and respondents indicate their relationship to the leader

(manager, coworker/peer, direct report, or other). Except for the manager, identification of the observers is anonymous. The LPI takes approximately 10 minutes to complete. Each behavioral statement uses a 10-point Likert scale, and a higher value represents more frequent use of a leadership behavior. The anchors for the scale are: (1) *Almost never* do what is described in the statement, (2) *Rarely,* (3) *Seldom,* (4) *Once in a while,* (5) *Occasionally,* (6) *Sometimes,* (7) *Fairly often,* (8) *Usually,* (9) *Very frequently,* and (10) *Almost always* do what is described in the statement. Scores on the five leadership practices can range from 6 to 60; scores on the overall LPI (combining all five practices) can range from 30 to 300.

The Five Practices framework and the LPI have been in use for more than 35 years, both in applied leadership development settings and in hundreds of research projects. More than 3.7 million people from over 200 countries have completed the LPI 360 Online; of these more than 575,000 are leaders, and the remainder are observers, including the leaders' managers, coworkers/peers, and direct reports. Using this online format provides access to a large, international sample comprising sincerely interested and committed participants who are engaging in natural behavior, rather than performing in the context of a research study. The LPI is a well-established means of conceptualizing leadership that has demonstrated applicability across settings and cultures.

Research that we and other researchers have conducted over the years consistently confirms the reliability and validity of the LPI and The Five Practices of Exemplary Leadership model. Reliability from a research perspective is about consistency or "repeatability." This means that the instrument (assessment, survey, questionnaire) would give the same result over and over again, assuming that what was being measured isn't changing. (Remember that reliability is a characteristic of a measure taken across individuals and doesn't speak to the reliability (consistency) of an individual.)

Scores will seldom, if ever, be 100 percent reliable (that is, identical) because of random errors (often referred to as "noise") that cause scores to differ for reasons unrelated to the individual respondent. The fewer errors contained, the more reliable the instrument. Instrument reliabilities above 0.60 are considered good; those above 0.80 are very strong. The internal reliabilities for the LPI, as measured by Cronbach alpha coefficients, are consistently strong and generally above 0.81.

Another consideration for examining the reliability of any instrument is how it might vary as a result of individual or organizational differences. The lack of systematic variations would indicate that the instrument is quite robust and would be safe (reliable) to apply across various sample population characteristics. All in all, LPI scores have been found to be independent of various demographic characteristics (e.g., age, marital status, years of experience, educational level, ethnicity) and organizational features (e.g., size, functional area, length of service, line versus staff position, industry).

Reliability is a first-order investigation of a framework or instrument and is necessary but not sufficient to determine whether one can be reasonably confident that it truly measures what it purports to measure and whether its scores (results) have meaning or utility for a respondent. From a practical perspective, this is the answer to the *so what?* question, as in, *So what difference do my scores make in terms of some substantive outcome?* This is called validity.

Like reliability, validity is determined in a number of ways. The most common assessment of validity is called *face validity,* which considers whether, on the basis of subjective evaluation, an instrument appears to measure what it intends to measure. Given that the items on the LPI are related to the qualitative findings from interviews with leaders and echo the comments that workshop and seminar participants generally make about their own or others' Personal-Best Leadership Experiences, respondents have found the LPI to have excellent face validity.

Validity is also determined empirically (objectively). Factor analysis is used to determine the extent to which the instrument items measure common or different content areas. The results from various analyses reveal that the LPI contains five factors, the items within each factor (representing a leadership practice) corresponding more among themselves than they do with the other factors.

The question of whether LPI scores are significantly related to other critical behavioral (individual and organizational) performance measures is probably the most important practical matter to leaders and their organizations. The answer to this issue is generally referred to as *predictive validity*. Scores of studies have shown that the leadership practices and behaviors measured by the LPI are consistently associated with important aspects of managerial and organizational effectiveness such as workgroup performance, team cohesiveness, commitment, satisfaction, and credibility.

Abstracts of more than 700 of these studies can be found on our website, leadershipchallenge.com/research, including more than 120 conducted within higher education. Among these are investigations of college presidents, academic deans and department chairs, librarians, counseling directors, and student personnel administrators. There are studies examining the impact of leadership practices on faculty job satisfaction, transformational leadership of athletic directors and head coaches, the relationship between leadership and emotional intelligence, the leadership effectiveness of residence hall directors, demographic differences of leadership practices within a historically black university, and so on. Moreover, researchers have looked at leadership in a variety of higher-education settings and environments; for example, public and private schools, secular and nonsecular campuses, two-year and four-year colleges, on-campus and online programs, as well as institutions inside and outside the United States.

In this book are specific references to the research most directly applicable to higher education. This data and analysis draw on a subsection of the Kouzes Posner normative LPI database, a sample of more than 125,000 people *in higher education* who completed the LPI and provided information about themselves and how they feel about their organization and their leaders. Each chapter includes data about the impact of leadership on people and how consistently the most effective leaders in higher education are the ones who make the most frequent use of The Five Practices.

In addition to the quantitative data, we collected Personal-Best Leadership Experience cases from more than 100 people in a variety of roles in higher education—president's office, campus safety, library, athletics, student activities, housing, public safety, alumni relations, health centers, and other campus organizations and functions. Their stories and case studies bring the data to life. They show you more specifically what exemplary leadership practices and behaviors look like and the positive impact they have. They illustrate that leadership is not something available to only a few select leaders in an institution. They are evidence that leadership is a set of skills and abilities available to everyone on campus.

We know from our research that the more frequently you put The Five Practices to use, the more effective you will be in bringing out the best in your group, department, and institution. The opportunity is there. The evidence is there. What remains, as we say in the closing of chapter 7, is: "Decide to do something different that will make you an even better leader. Then hop off the log and get into the water!"

Notes

Preface

1. Brent D. Ruben, Richard De Lisi, and Ralph A. Gigliotti, *A Guide for Leaders in Higher Education: Core Concepts, Competencies, and Tools* (Sterling, VA: Stylus, 2017).

2. Goldie Blumenstyk, *American Higher Education in Crisis? What Everyone Needs to Know* (New York: Oxford University Press, 2015).

3. Barry Z. Posner, "It's How Leaders Behave That Matters, Not Where They Are From," *Leadership & Organization Development Journal* 34, no. 6 (2013): 573–87, https://doi.org/10.1108/LODJ-11-2011-0115.

4. James M. Kouzes and Barry Z. Posner, *The Leadership Challenge: How to Make Extraordinary Things Happen in Organizations,* 6th ed. (Hoboken, NJ: John Wiley & Sons, 2017).

CHAPTER **1**
Leadership Is a Relationship

1. Alexander W. Astin and Helen S. Astin, *Leadership Reconsidered: Engaging Higher Education in Social Change* (Battle Creek, MI: W. K. Kellogg Foundation, 2000).

2. World Economic Forum, *The Future of Jobs: Employment, Skills and Workforce Strategy for the Fourth Industrial Revolution* (Geneva, Switzerland: World Economic Forum, January 2016), http://www3.weforum.org/docs/WEF_Future_of_Jobs.pdf.

3. Barry Z. Posner, "On Putting Theory into Practice," *Journal of Management Inquiry* 18, no. 2 (2009): 139–41, https://doi.org/10.1177/1056492608326321.

4. Margaret Bauer, "Are the Leadership Practices of College Presidents in the Northeast Distinct from Those of Business and Industry?" (PhD diss., University of New Haven, December 1993); Phillip H. Broome, "The Relationship between Perceptions of Presidential Leadership Practices and Organizational Effectiveness in Southern Community Colleges" (PhD diss., University of Mississippi [Oxford], May 2003); Randi Dikeman, "Leadership Practices and Leadership Ethics of North Carolina Community College Presidents" (PhD diss., East Carolina University, October 2007); and Christine D. Hempowicz, "Transformational Leadership Characteristics of College and University Presidents of Private, Title III and Title V–Eligible Institutions" (PhD diss., University of Bridgeport, April 2010).

5. Susan Stephenson, "Promoting Teamwork: Leadership Attitudes and Other Characteristics of a Community College Chief Financial Officer" (PhD diss., University of Arkansas, May 2002).

6. Zin Lin Xu, "The Relationship between Leadership Behavior of Academic Deans in Public Universities and Job Satisfaction of Department Chairpersons" (PhD diss., East Tennessee State University, May 1991); Jesus R. Castro, "Effective Leadership among Academic Deans: An Exploration of the Relationships between Emotional Competence and Leadership Effectiveness" (PhD diss., University of Missouri [Columbia], May 2003); Mary J. Harris, "Characteristics, Behaviors, and Preparation for Leadership of Educational Administration/Leadership Department Chairs" (PhD diss., University of Missouri [Columbia], December 2004; Jaime Kleim and Becky Takeda-Tinker, "The Impact of Leadership on Community College Faculty Job Satisfaction," *Academic Leadership* 7, no. 2 (2009): 1–5, https://scholars .fhsu.edu/cgi/viewcontent.cgi?article=1293&context=alj.

7. Carolyn Y. Brightharp, "Real and Ideal Leadership Practices of Women in Mid-Level Administrative Positions in Student Affairs" (PhD diss., Bowling Green State University, December 1999); Aparajita Maitra, "An Analysis of Leadership Styles and Practices of University Women in Administrative Vice Presidencies" (PhD diss., Bowling Green State University, August 2007); David J. Rozeboom, "Self-Report and Direct Observer's Perceived Leadership Practices of Chief Student Affairs Officers in Selected Institutions of Higher Education in the United States" (PhD diss., Texas A&M University, August 2008); Jeffrey L. Kegolis, "New Professionals' Perspectives of Supervision in Student Affairs" (PhD diss., Bowling Green State University,

May 2009); and Melaine L. Davenport, "Examining the Relationships of Perceptions of Leadership Behaviors, Self-Efficacy and Job Satisfaction of University and College Counseling Center Directors: Implications for Strengthening Leadership Training" (PhD diss., University of Maryland Eastern Shore, November 2011).

8. Russell D. Elliott, "Identifying and Analyzing the Practices Utilized by Coaches in Achieving Their 'Personal Best' in Coaching" (master's thesis, Iowa State University, June 1990); Jodi P. Coffman, "The Community College Coach: Leadership Practices and Athlete Satisfaction" (PhD diss., University of San Diego, April 1999); Leslie S. Danehy, "The Relationship between Emotional Intelligence and Leadership in NCAA Division III College Coaches" (PhD diss., Wilmington College, December 2005); and Elaine J. Dispo, "On the Field and Outside the Lines: Relationships between Student-Athletes' Perceptions of Their Intercollegiate Coaches' Leadership Practices and Student-Athletes' Self- Reported Satisfaction, Athletic and Academic Performance" (PhD diss., Our Lady of the Lake University, December 2015).

9. Kimberly A. Hirsh, "The Transformational Leadership Practices of National Board Certified School Librarians in North Carolina" (PhD diss., University of North Carolina [Chapel Hill], April 2011); and Daniella Smith, "School District Support Services: A Mixed Methods Study of the Leadership Development of Pre-Service School Librarians," *School Libraries Worldwide* 21, no. 2 (2015): 58–73.

10. Federico Solis, "A Profile of Faculty Leadership Behavior at One South Texas Community College" (PhD diss., Texas A&M University, May 2011); E. Quinn, "Demographical Differences in Perceptions of Leadership Practices for Department Chairs and Job Satisfaction of Faculty Members at a Historically Black University" (PhD diss., Argosy University [Atlanta], March 2012); and Melissa M. Bryant, "Leadership Practices among Undergraduate Nursing Instructors" (PhD diss., University of Southern Mississippi, May 2015).

11. All the empirical analyses reported in this book, unless indicated otherwise, use only respondents in the Kouzes Posner normative LPI database from higher education. The responses from "direct reports" are used to provide a relatively independent view of the leaders' actual behavior and because they are the people whom leaders have to most influence to achieve the

objectives and goals of their units. Here are some of the specific statements to which direct reports responded:

> "My workgroup has a strong sense of team spirit."
> "I am proud to tell others that I work for this organization."
> "I am committed to this organization's success."
> "I would work harder and for longer hours if the job demanded it."
> "I am highly productive in my job."
> "I am clear about what is expected of me in my job."
> "I feel that my organization values my work."
> "I am effective in meeting the demands of my job."
> "Around my workplace, people seem to trust management."
> "I feel like I am making a difference in this organization."
> "Overall this individual [in reference to the person who asked you to complete this survey] is an effective leader."

All responses used a five-point Likert scale with the following anchors: (1) Strongly disagree, (2) Disagree, (3) Neither agree nor disagree, (4) Agree, and (5) Strongly agree.

12. James M. Kouzes and Barry Z. Posner, *Credibility: How Leaders Gain and Lose It, Why People Demand It,* 2nd ed. (Hoboken, NJ: John Wiley & Sons, 2011).

13. James M. Kouzes and Barry Z. Posner, *The Leadership Challenge: How to Make Extraordinary Things Happen in Organizations,* 6th ed. (Hoboken, NJ: John Wiley & Sons, 2017).

14. Barry Z. Posner, "The Influence of Demographic Factors on What People Want from Their Leaders," *Journal of Leadership Studies* 12, no. 2 (2018): 7–16, https://doi.org/10.1002/jls.21553.

15. The classic study on credibility goes back to Carl I. Hovland, Irving L. Janis, and Harold H. Kelley, *Communication and Persuasion: Psychological Studies of Opinion Change* (New Haven, CT: Yale University Press, 1953). Early measurement studies include James C. McCroskey, "Scales for the Measurement of Ethos," *Speech Monographs* 33, no. 1 (1966): 65–72, https://doi.org/10.1080/03637756609375482; and David K. Berlo, James B. Lemert, and Robert J. Mertz, "Dimensions for Evaluating the Acceptability of Message Sources," *Public Opinion Quarterly* 3, no 4 (1969): 563–76, https://doi

.org/10.1086/267745. Even further back, however, writing in the *Rhetoric,* Aristotle (384–322 BCE) suggested that ethos—the trust of a speaker by the listener, or what some have referred to as "source credibility"—was based on the listener's perception of three characteristics of the speaker: the intelligence of the speaker (correctness of opinions, or competence), the character of the speaker (reliability, a competence factor, and honesty, a measure of intentions), and the goodwill of the speaker (positive energy and favorable intentions toward the listener). These three characteristics—competence, honesty, and inspiration—have consistently emerged in factor-analytic investigations of communicator credibility (Daniel J. O'Keefe, *Persuasion: Theory and Research* [Thousand Oaks, CA: Sage, 2002]). Another contemporary perspective is provided in Robert B. Cialdini, *Influence: The Psychology of Persuasion* (New York: Harper Business, 2006).

CHAPTER **2**

Model the Way

1. Deryl R. Leaming, "Academic Deans," in *Field Guide to Academic Leadership,* ed. Robert M. Diamond (San Francisco: Jossey-Bass, 2002), 438.

2. Leaming, "Academic Deans," 438.

3. Tammy Stone and Mary Coussons-Read, *Leading from the Middle: A Case-Study Approach to Academic Leadership for Associate Deans* (Lanham, MD: Rowman & Littlefield, 2011).

4. For example, see: Jeffrey L. Buller, *Positive Academic Leadership: How to Stop Putting Out Fires and Start Making a Difference* (San Francisco: Jossey-Bass, 2013); and William A. Gentry and Taylor E. Sparks, "A Convergence/ Divergence Perspective of Leadership Competencies Managers Believe Are Most Important for Success in Organizations: A Cross-Cultural Multilevel Analysis of 40 Countries," *Journal of Business and Psychology* 27, no. 1 (2012): 15–30, http://dx.doi.org/10.1007/s10869-011-9212-y.

5. Chip Daniels, "Developing Organizational Values in Others," in *Leadership Lessons from West Point,* ed. Doug Crandall (San Francisco: Jossey-Bass, 2007), 62–87; and Ann Rhoads and Nancy Shepherdson, *Built on Values: Creating an Enviable Culture That Outperforms the Competition* (San Francisco: Jossey-Bass, 2011).

6. Barry Z. Posner, "Another Look at the Impact of Personal and Organizational Values Congruency," *Journal of Business Ethics* 97, no. 4 (2010): 535-41, https://doi.org/10.1007/s10551-010-0530-1.

7. Judith A. Ramaley, "Moving Mountains: Institutional Culture and Transformational Change," in *Field Guide to Academic Leadership,* ed. Robert M. Diamond (San Francisco: Jossey-Bass, 2002) 59–73.

8. Stephen Denning, *The Springboard: How Storytelling Ignites Action in Knowledge-Era Organizations* (Boston: Butterworth-Heinemann, 2001); and Douglas A. Ready, "How Storytelling Builds Next-Generation Leaders," *MIT Sloan Management Review,* July 15, 2002, 63–69.

9. Shoshana Zuboff, *In the Age of the Smart Machine: The Future of Work and Power* (New York: Basic Books, 1988), 394.

10. Hal B. Gregersen, *Questions Are the Answer: A Breakthrough Approach to Your Most Vexing Problems at Work and in Life* (New York: HarperBusiness, 2018).

CHAPTER **3**

Inspire a Shared Vision

1. Catherine Bailey and Adrian Madden, "What Makes Work Meaningful—or Meaningless," *MIT Sloan Management Review,* June 1, 2016, 52–61, http://sro.sussex.ac.uk/id/eprint/61282/1/What%20makes%20work%20meaningful%20or%20meaningless%20accepted%20version.pdf.

2. Jean Case, *Be Fearless: 5 Principles for a Life of Breakthroughs and Purpose* (New York: Simon & Schuster, 2019).

3. See: Daniel Kahneman, *Thinking, Fast and Slow* (New York: Farrar, Straus and Giroux, 2011); Hugo Mercier and Dan Sperber, *The Enigma of Reason* (Cambridge, MA: Harvard University Press, 2017); and Lea Kosnik, "Refusing to Budge: A Confirmatory Bias in Decision Making? *Mind & Society* 7, no. 2 (2018): 193–214.

4. David E. Berlew, "Leadership and Organizational Excitement," *California Management Review* 17, no. 2 (1974): 21–30, https://doi.org/10.2307/41164557; and Robert M. Diamond, ed., *Field Guide to Academic Leadership* (San Francisco: Jossey-Bass, 2002).

5. Hay Group, "The Retention Dilemma" (working paper), 2001; and Ann F. Lucas, "A Teamwork Approach to Change in the Academic Department," in Ann F. Lucas and Associates, *Leading Academic Change: Essential Roles for Department Chairs* (San Francisco: Jossey-Bass, 2000), 7–32.

6. Peter M. Senge, *The Fifth Discipline: The Art and Practice of the Learning Organization* (New York: Doubleday, 1990), 206.

7. Parker J. Palmer, *Let Your Life Speak: Listening for the Voice of Vocation* (San Francisco: Jossey-Bass, 2000).

8. Danuek Goleman, *Social Intelligence: The New Science of Human Relationships* (New York: Bantam, 2006).

9. Barbara L. Fredrickson, *Positivity: Top-Notch Research Reveals the 3-to-1 Ratio That Will Change Your Life* (New York: Crown, 2009); and Jeffrey L. Buller, *Positive Academic Leadership: How to Stop Putting Out Fires and Start Making a Difference* (San Francisco: Jossey-Bass, 2013).

10. Bernard M. Bass, *Leadership and Performance beyond Expectations* (New York: Free Press, 1985), 35.

11. Daniel Goleman, Richard E. Boyatzis, and Annie McKee, *Primal Leadership: Realizing the Power of Emotional Intelligence* (Boston: Harvard Business Review Press, 2002); and Jay A. Conger, *Winning 'Em Over: A New Management Model in the Age of Persuasion* (New York: Simon & Schuster, 1998).

12. Belle Linda Halpern and Kathy Lubar, *Leadership Presence: Dramatic Techniques to Reach Out, Motivate, and Inspire* (New York: Gotham Books, 2003).

CHAPTER **4**

Challenge the Process

1. Jeffrey L. Buller, *Positive Academic Leadership: How to Stop Putting Out Fires and Start Making a Difference* (San Francisco: Jossey-Bass, 2013), 50.

2. Albert Bandura, *Self-Efficacy: The Exercise of Control* (New York: W. H. Freeman, 1997); and Jeffrey A. LePine and Linn Van Dyne, "Predicting Voice Behavior in Work Groups," *Journal of Applied Psychology* 83, no. 6 (1998): 853–68, http://dx.doi.org/10.1037/0021-9010.83.6.853.

3. Kay J. Gillespie and Douglas L. Robertson, *A Guide to Faculty Development*, 2nd ed. (San Francisco: Jossey-Bass, 2010).

4. Edward L. Deci, *Intrinsic Motivation* (New York: Plenum Press, 1975); and Daniel H. Pink, *Drive: The Surprising Truth about What Motivates Us* (New York: Riverhead Books, 2009).

5. Margaret J. Wheatley, *Leadership and the New Science: Learning about Organization from an Orderly Universe* (San Francisco: Berrett-Koehler, 1992).

6. Jeffrey H. Dyer, Hal Gregersen, and Clayton M. Christensen, "The Innovator's DNA," *Harvard Business Review* 87, no. 2 (2009): 60–67, https://hbr.org/2009/12/the-innovators-dna.

7. Peter Sims, *Little Bets: How Breakthrough Ideas Emerge from Small Discoveries* (New York: Simon & Schuster, 2011).

8. This approach is also used by start-up entrepreneurs outside higher education. For example, see Eric Ries, *The Lean Startup: How Today's Entrepreneurs Use Continuous Innovation to Create Radically Successful Businesses* (New York: Crown Business, 2011).

9. Henry Mintzberg, *The Rise and Fall of Strategic Planning: Reconceiving Roles for Planning, Plans, Planners* (New York: Free Press, 1994).

10. Karl E. Weick, "Small Wins: Redefining the Scale of Social Problems," *American Psychologist* 39, no. 1 (1984): 40–49.

11. Angela Duckworth, Christopher Peterson, Michael D. Matthews, et al., "Grit: Perseverance and Passion for Long-Term Goals," *Journal of Personality and Social Psychology* 92, no. 6 (2007): 1087–1101. Also see Angela Duckworth, *Grit: The Power of Passion and Perseverance* (New York: Scribner, 2016).

12. Arran Caza and Barry Z. Posner, "How and When Does Grit Influence Leaders' Behavior?" *Leadership & Organization Development Journal* 40, no. 1 (2019): 124–34, https://doi.org/10.1108/LODJ-06-2018-0209.

13. See Salvatore R. Maddi, "The Story of Hardiness: Twenty Years of Theorizing, Research, and Practice," *Consulting Psychology Journal: Practices and Research* 54, no. 3 (2002): 175–85. Also see: Salvatore R. Maddi and Suzanne Kobasa, *The Hardy Executive: Health Under Stress* (Chicago: Dorsey Press, 1984); Salvatore R. Maddi and Deborah M. Khoshaba, "Hardiness and

Mental Health," *Journal of Personality Assessment* 63, no. 2 (1994): 265–74, http://dx.doi.org/10.1207/s15327752jpa6302_6; and Salvatore R. Maddi and Deborah M. Khoshaba, *Resilience at Work: How to Succeed No Matter What Life Throws at You* (New York: MJF Books, 2005).

14. See: Reginald A. Bruce and Robert F. Sinclair, "Exploring the Psychological Hardiness of Entrepreneurs," *Frontiers of Entrepreneurship Research* 29, no. 6 (2009): 5; Paul T. Bartone, Robert R. Roland, James J. Picano, et al., "Psychological Hardiness Predicts Success in U.S. Army Special Forces Candidates," *International Journal of Selection and Assessment* 16, no. 1 (2008): 78–81; Paul T. Bartone, "Resilience Under Military Operational Stress: Can Leaders Influence Hardiness?" *Military Psychology* 18 (suppl.) (2006), S141–S148, http://www.hardiness-resilience.com/docs/Bartone .pdf; and Caza and Posner, "How and When Does Grit Influence Leaders' Behavior?"

CHAPTER **5**

Enable Others to Act

1. Michael B. Gurtman, "Trust, Distrust, and Interpersonal Problems: A Circumplex Analysis," *Journal of Personality and Social Psychology* 62, no. 6 (1992): 989–1002, http://dx.doi.org/10.1037/0022-3514.62.6.989; and Glenn D. Grace and Thomas Schill, "Social Support and Coping Style Differences in Subjects High and Low in Interpersonal Trust," *Psychological Reports* 59, no. 2 (part 1) (1986): 584–86.

2. James W. Driscoll, "Trust and Participation in Organizational Decision-Making as Predictors of Satisfaction," *Academy of Management Journal* 21 (1978): 44–56, https://doi.org/10.1177/105960117800300422.

3. Lionel Tiger, "Real-Life Survivors Rely on Teamwork," *Wall Street Journal*, August 25, 2000, B7.

4. William Poundstone, *Prisoner's Dilemma: John von Neumann, Game Theory, and the Puzzle of the Bomb* (New York: Doubleday, 1992).

5. Robert B. Cialdini, *Influence: Science and Practice*, 4th ed. (Needham Heights, MA: Allyn & Bacon, 2000), 19–51.

6. David W. Johnson and Roger T. Johnson, *Cooperation and Competition: Theory and Research* (Edina, MN: Interaction Book Company, 1989).

7. Wayne E. Baker, *Achieving Success through Social Capital: Tapping the Hidden Resources in Your Personal and Business Networks* (San Francisco: Jossey-Bass, 2000).

8. Don Cohen and Laurence Prusak, *In Good Company: How Social Capital Makes Organizations Work* (Boston: Harvard Business School Press, 2001).

9. Marcus Buckingham and Curt Coffman, *First, Break All the Rules: What the World's Greatest Managers Do Differently* (New York: Simon & Schuster, 1999); and Gallup, *State of the Global Workplace* (New York: Gallup Press, 2017).

10. Susan Rebstock Williams and Rick L. Wilson, "Group Support Systems, Power, and Influence in an Organization: A Field Study," *Decision Sciences* 28, no. 4 (1997): 911–37; Patty Azzarello, "Why Sharing Power at Work Is the Very Best Way to Build It," *Fast Company,* January 18, 2013, https://www.fastcompany.com/3004867/why-sharing-power-work-very-best-way-build-it; and Edward L. Deci, Anja H. Olafsen, and Richard M. Ryan, "Self-Determination Theory in Work Organizations: The State of a Science," *Annual Review of Organizational Psychology and Organizational Behavior* 4 (2017): 19–43, https://doi.org/10.1146/annurev-orgpsych-032516-113108.

11. Patrick J. Sweeney, Vaida Thompson, and Hart Blanton, "Trust and Influence in Combat: An Interdependence Model," *Journal of Applied Social Psychology* 39, no. 1 (2009): 235–64, http://dx.doi.org/10.1111/j.1559-1816.2008.00437.x.

12. Michael Burchell and Jennifer Robin, *The Great Workplace: How to Build It, How to Keep It, and Why It Matters* (San Francisco: Jossey-Bass, 2011), 66.

13. Robert Wood and Albert Bandura, "Impact of Conceptions of Ability on Self-Regulatory Mechanisms and Complex Decision Making," *Journal of Personality and Social Psychology* 56, no. 3 (1989): 407–15.

CHAPTER **6**
Encourage the Heart

1. Amy Zipkin, "Management: The Wisdom of Thoughtfulness," *New York Times,* May 31, 2000, https://www.nytimes.com/2000/05/31/business/management-the-wisdom-of-thoughtfulness.html.

2. Mihaly Csikszentmihalyi, *Finding Flow: The Psychology of Engagement with Everyday Life* (New York: Basic Books, 1997).

3. See: John E. Sawyer, William R. Latham, Robert D. Pritchard, et al., "Analysis of Work Group Productivity in an Applied Setting: Application of a Time Series Panel Design," *Personnel Psychology* 52, no. 4 (1999): 927–67, https://doi.org/10.1111/j.1744-6570.1999.tb00185.x; Adrian Gostick and Chester Elton, *Managing with Carrots: Using Recognition to Attract and Retain the Best People* (Layton, UT: Gibbs Smith, 2001); John Hattie and Helen Timperley, "The Power of Feedback," *Review of Educational Research* 77, no. 1 (2007): 81–112, https://doi.org/10.3102%2F003465430298487; and Susan J. Ashford and Kathleen E. M. De Stobbeleir, "Feedback, Goal Setting, and Task Performance Revisited," *New Developments in Goal Setting and Task Performance,* eds. Edwin A. Locke and Gary P. Latham (New York: Routledge, 2013), 51–64.

4. Paulette A. McCarty, "Effects of Feedback on the Self-Confidence of Men and Women," *Academy of Management Journal* 29, no. 4 (1986): 840–47, https://doi.org/10.5465/255950.

5. Alison E. Smith, Lee Jussim, Jacquelynne Eccles, et al., "Self-Fulfilling Prophecies, Perceptual Biases, and Accuracy at the Individual and Group Levels," *Journal of Experimental Social Psychology* 34, no. 6 (1998): 530–61, https://pdfs.semanticscholar.org/b900/9f21ed9064f59ac71e02bdad2dbc33f4f728.pdf; and Dov Eden, "Leadership and Expectations: Pygmalion Effects and Other Self-Fulfilling Prophecies in Organizations," *The Leadership Quarterly* 3, no. 4 (1992): 271–305, https://doi.org/10.1016/1048-9843(92)90018-B.

6. Roy J. Blitzer, Colleen Petersen, and Linda Rogers, "How to Build Self-Esteem," *Training and Development Journal* 47, no. 2 (1993): 59; also see Barry L. Reece and Monique Reece, *Effective Human Relations: Interpersonal and Organizational Applications,* 13th ed. (Boston: Cengage Learning, 2017).

7. Kim S. Cameron, *Positive Leadership: Strategies for Extraordinary Performance* (San Francisco: Berrett-Koehler, 2008).

8. David L. Cooperrider, "Positive Image, Positive Action: The Affirmative Basis of Organizing," in Suresh Srivastva and David L. Cooperrider, *Appreciative Management and Leadership: The Power of Positive Thought and Action in Organizations* (San Francisco: Jossey-Bass, 1990), 103.

9. Cooperrider, "Positive Image, Positive Action," 114.

10. Carol S. Dweck, *Mindset: The New Psychology of Success* (New York: Ballantine Books, 2006); David Scott Yeager and Carol S. Dweck, "Mindsets That Promote Resilience: When Students Believe That Personal Characteristics Can Be Developed," *Educational Psychologist* 47, no. 4 (2012): 302–14, https://doi.org/10.1080/00461520.2012.722805; and David Scott Yeager, Rebecca Johnson, Brian James Spitzer, et al., "The Far-Reaching Effects of Believing People Can Change: Implicit Theories of Personality Shape Stress, Health, and Achievement During Adolescence," *Journal of Personality and Social Psychology* 106, no. 6 (2014): 867–84, https://doi.org/10.1037/a0036335.

11. Tae Kyung Kouzes and Barry Z. Posner, "Influence of the Leader's Mindset on Leadership Behavior" (working paper, Leavey School of Business, Santa Clara University, 2019).

12. Terrence E. Deal and M. K. Key, *Corporate Celebration: Play, Purpose, and Profit at Work* (San Francisco: Berrett-Koehler, 1998).

13. Ron Carucci, "What Not to Do When You're Trying to Motivate Your Team," *Harvard Business Review,* July 16, 2018, https://hbr.org/2018/07/what-not-to-do-when-youre-trying-to-motivate-your-team.

14. Bob Nelson, *1001 Ways to Reward Employees,* 2nd ed. (New York: Workman, 2005).

15. O. C. Tannner Learning Group, *Performance: Accelerated: A New Benchmark for Initiating Employee Engagement, Retention and Results* (white paper), https://www.octanner.com/content/dam/oc-tanner/documents/global-research/White_Paper_Performance_Accelerated.pdf.

16. James T. Bond, Ellen Galinsky, and Jennifer E. Swanberg, *The National Study of the Changing Workforce, 1997* (New York: Families and Work Institute, 1998).

17. Robert Nelson, "The Power of Rewards and Recognition" (presentation to the Consortium on Executive Education, Leavey School of Business, Santa Clara University, September 20, 1996).

18. O. C. Tannner Learning Group, *Performance: Accelerated.*

19. Leonard L. Berry, A. Parasuraman, Valarie A. Zeithaml, et al., "Improving Service Quality in America: Lessons Learned [and Executive Commentary]," *Academy of Management Executive* 8, no. 2 (1994): 32–52, https://www.jstor .org/stable/4165187.

20. Tom Rath, *Vital Friends: The People You Can't Afford to Live Without* (New York: Gallup Press, 2006), 52. For an update on this research, see also Tom Rath and Jim Harter, *Wellbeing: The Five Essential Elements* (New York: Gallup Press, 2010), 40–43. For a follow-up report on the Gallup engagement research, including a discussion of the importance of having friends in the workplace, see Rodd Wagner and James K. Harter, *12: The Elements of Great Managing* (New York: Gallup Press, 2006).

21. Gary A. Klein, *Sources of Power: How People Make Decisions* (Cambridge, MA: MIT Press, 1998). For more on the importance of storytelling and decision-making, see: Gary Klein, *The Power of Intuition: How to Use Your Gut Feelings to Make Better Decisions at Work* (New York: Currency Books, 2004); and Gary Klein, *Streetlights and Shadows: Searching for the Keys to Adaptive Decision Making* (Boston: MIT Press, 2009).

CHAPTER **7**

Leadership Is Everyone's Business

1. James M. Kouzes and Barry Z. Posner, *The Truth about Leadership: The No-Fads, Heart-of-the-Matter Facts You Need to Know* (San Francisco: Jossey-Bass, 2010).

2. James M. Kouzes and Barry Z. Posner, *Learning Leadership: The Five Fundamentals of Becoming an Exemplary Leader* (San Francisco: Wiley, 2016).

3. For more on humility, see: Rob Nielsen, Jennifer A. Marrone, and Holly S. Ferraro, *Leading with Humility* (New York: Routledge, 2014); Bradley P. Owens and David R. Hekman, "How Does Leader Humility Influence Team Performance? Exploring the Mechanisms of Contagion and Collective Promotion Focus," *Academy of Management Journal* 59, no. 3 (2016): 1088–111, https://doi.org/10.5465/amj.2013.0660; Edgar H. Schein and Peter Schein, *Humble Leadership: The Power of Relationships, Openness, and Trust* (Oakland, CA: Berrett-Koehler, 2018); and Rob Nielsen and Jennifer A. Marrone, "Humility: Our Current Understanding of the Construct and

Its Role in Organizations," *International Journal of Management Reviews* 20, no. 4 (2018): 805–24, https://doi.org/10.1111/ijmr.12160.

4. Liz Wiseman, *Multipliers: How the Best Leaders Make Everyone Smarter* (New York: HarperBusiness, 2017).

5. Jim Collins, *Good to Great: Why Some Companies Make the Leap…and Others Don't* (New York: HarperCollins, 2001), 27.

6. T. Bradford Bitterly, Alison Wood Brooks, and Maurice E. Schweitzer, "Risky Business: When Humor Increases and Decreases Status," *Journal of Personality and Social Psychology* 112, no. 3 (2017): 431–55, http://dx.doi .org/10.1037/pspi0000079.

7. C. R. Snyder, *The Psychology of Hope: You Can Get There from Here* (New York, Free Press, 1994); Shane J. Lopez, *Making Hope Happen: Create the Future You Want for Yourself and Others* (New York: Simon & Schuster, 2013); and Nir Halevy, "Preemptive Strikes: Fear, Hope, and Defensive Aggression," *Journal of Personality and Social Psychology* 112, no. 2 (2017): 224–37, http://dx.doi.org/10.1037/pspi0000077.

Acknowledgments

THERE IS ALWAYS A LONG LIST OF PEOPLE TO THANK and credit when anything special is accomplished, as well there should be. Leadership is not a solo performance, nor is writing about it.

First, we once again acknowledge and give thanks to the many people who have been with us through scores of leadership projects, programs, and publications over the past three decades. We devoted nearly four pages to mentioning their names in the acknowledgment section of *The Leadership Challenge* (6th edition) and continue to carry a deep debt of gratitude for all the gracious support and encouragement we've received.

Second, we want to single out and recognize a number of special people who made significant contributions to this book: Prashnath Asuri, Evan Cree Gee, Lillas Marie Hatala, Barry Johansen, Cheryl Johnson, Nicholas Lopez, Donna Perry, Lori Ann Roth, Todd Sutherland, and Halley Sutton.

A very special thanks to our colleagues at Berrett-Koehler, who supported us throughout the process of writing, editing, and producing *Leadership in Higher Education*. Foremost is Steve Piersanti, our editor and the person who signed our first book contract more than 30 years ago. Steve championed this book, and we are grateful to him for his wise advice and counsel. We sincerely appreciate the care, attention, and professionalism of Courtney Schonfeld, Berrett-Koehler's senior manager of production and audio; Valerie Caldwell, associate director of design and production; and Mike Crowley, associate director of sales and marketing. Elizabeth von Radics applied her editorial services and mastery of the language to strengthen the readability of this work. And through his design craftsmanship and artistic sensibilities, Gary Palmatier of Ideas and Images created the appealing look and feel of the interior pages.

Finally, here's to every faculty member, university staffer, and college administrator who contributed directly or indirectly to whatever we know, and have learned, about leading in higher-education settings and situations. You were there for us when we experimented, when we tried and succeeded, and when we missed the mark and needed to try again. Whatever we learned and accomplished, we couldn't have done it alone. Many thanks.

Index

Page locators in *italics* refer to figures.

About the Authors

Jim Kouzes   Barry Posner

JIM KOUZES AND BARRY POSNER together have been involved with higher-education administration for more than 50 years.

Jim founded the Joint Center for Human Services Development at San José State University and directed the Executive Development Center at Santa Clara University. He's currently an Executive Fellow at the Center for Innovation and Entrepreneurship at the Leavey School of Business at Santa Clara University and is a Fellow of the Doerr Institute for New Leaders at Rice University. Jim can be reached via email at jim@kouzes.com.

Barry currently holds the Michael J. Accolti, S.J., Chair, and is a professor of leadership at the Leavey School of Business at Santa Clara University. He has been associate dean for graduate programs and a managing partner for executive education, and he served as dean for 12 years. Barry can be reached via email at bposner@scu.edu.

Jim and Barry are recipients of the prestigious Wilbur M. McFeely Award, given to the nation's top leadership educators by the International Management Council, and the Association for Talent Development's highest award for Distinguished Contribution to Workplace Learning and Performance. They have been recognized among the Top 50 Leadership Coaches in America, ranked among the Most

Influential HR Thinkers in the World by *HR* magazine, listed among the Top 75 Leadership and Management Experts in the World by *Inc.* magazine, and among Global Gurus Top 20 Leadership Gurus!

They have provided leadership education programs on college campuses across the United States and around the globe, including such schools as California State University (CSU) Northridge; CSU Sacramento; CSU Sonoma; College of St. Thomas; Cornerstone University; Curtain University (Australia); Foothill–De Anza Community College District; Francisco Marroquín University (Guatemala); Gavilan College; Gonzaga University; Harper College; Harvard College; Hong Kong University of Science and Technology; Kent State University; Lingnan University (Hong Kong); Mt. San Antonio College; Mt. San Jacinto College; Pepperdine University; Queen's University (Canada); Royal Roads University (Canada); Sabancı University (Turkey); Saint Joseph's University; Simon Fraser University (Canada); Stanford University; Texas State University; United States Coast Guard Academy; University College Dublin (Ireland); University of Calgary (Canada); University of California (UC) Berkeley; UC Riverside; UC San Diego; UC Santa Barbara; UC Santa Cruz; University of Cincinnati; University of Dayton; University of Denver; University of La Verne; University of Massachusetts; University of Minnesota; University of Nevada, Reno; University of North Texas; University of Saskatchewan (Canada); University of South Carolina; University of Southern Maine; University of Texas at Austin; University of Texas at El Paso; University of Western Australia; Umpqua Community College; Utah State University; Western New England University; and Willamette University.

They have also conducted workshops and made keynote presentations for the Association of Fraternity/Sorority Advisors, Association to Advance Collegiate Schools of Business, California Business–Higher Education Forum, Canadian Association of University Business Officers, Community College League of California, National Association for Campus Activities, National Association of Student Personnel Administrators, Pacific Association of Collegiate Registrars and Admissions Officers, The Chair Academy, and the Western Association of College and University Business Officers.

Jim and Barry are coauthors of the award-winning book *The Leadership Challenge,* with more than 2.5 million copies in print. This book has been listed among the "Top 100 Business Books of All Time," receiving book-of-the-year honors from the American Council of Healthcare Executives, *Fast Company,* and the Critics' Choice Award from the nation's book review editors.

They have also written other award-winning, inspiring, and practical books on leadership, including: *Stop Selling and Start Leading: How to Make Extraordinary Sales Happen; Learning Leadership: The Five Fundamentals of Becoming an Exemplary Leader; Turning Adversity into Opportunity; Finding the Courage to Lead; Great Leadership Creates Great Workplaces; Credibility: How Leaders Gain and Lose It, Why People Demand It; The Truth about Leadership: The No-Fads, Heart-of-the-Matter Facts You Need to Know; Encouraging the Heart: A Leader's Guide to Rewarding and Recognizing Others; A Leader's Legacy; Extraordinary Leadership in Australia and New Zealand: The Five Practices That Create Great Workplaces; Making Extraordinary Things Happen in Asia: Applying The Five Practices of Exemplary Leadership;* and *The Student Leadership Challenge: Five Practices for Becoming an Exemplary Leader.*

Jim and Barry developed the widely used and highly acclaimed *Leadership Practices Inventory,* a 360-degree questionnaire assessing leadership behavior. The LPI has been completed by more than 5 million people around the globe. Over 700 doctoral dissertations and academic research projects have been based on The Five Practices of Exemplary Leadership framework. For more about all of Jim and Barry's publications and research, visit leadershipchallenge.com.

Berrett–Koehler
BK Publishers

Berrett-Koehler is an independent publisher dedicated to an ambitious mission: *Connecting people and ideas to create a world that works for all.*

Our publications span many formats, including print, digital, audio, and video. We also offer online resources, training, and gatherings. And we will continue expanding our products and services to advance our mission.

We believe that the solutions to the world's problems will come from all of us, working at all levels: in our society, in our organizations, and in our own lives. Our publications and resources offer pathways to creating a more just, equitable, and sustainable society. They help people make their organizations more humane, democratic, diverse, and effective (and we don't think there's any contradiction there). And they guide people in creating positive change in their own lives and aligning their personal practices with their aspirations for a better world.

And we strive to practice what we preach through what we call "The BK Way." At the core of this approach is *stewardship,* a deep sense of responsibility to administer the company for the benefit of all of our stakeholder groups, including authors, customers, employees, investors, service providers, sales partners, and the communities and environment around us. Everything we do is built around stewardship and our other core values of *quality, partnership, inclusion,* and *sustainability.*

This is why Berrett-Koehler is the first book publishing company to be both a B Corporation (a rigorous certification) and a benefit corporation (a for-profit legal status), which together require us to adhere to the highest standards for corporate, social, and environmental performance. And it is why we have instituted many pioneering practices (which you can learn about at www.bkconnection.com), including the Berrett-Koehler Constitution, the Bill of Rights and Responsibilities for BK Authors, and our unique Author Days.

We are grateful to our readers, authors, and other friends who are supporting our mission. We ask you to share with us examples of how BK publications and resources are making a difference in your lives, organizations, and communities at www.bkconnection.com/impact.

Dear reader,

Thank you for picking up this book and welcome to the worldwide BK community! You're joining a special group of people who have come together to create positive change in their lives, organizations, and communities.

What's BK all about?

Our mission is to connect people and ideas to create a world that works for all.

Why? Our communities, organizations, and lives get bogged down by old paradigms of self-interest, exclusion, hierarchy, and privilege. But we believe that can change. That's why we seek the leading experts on these challenges—and share their actionable ideas with you.

A welcome gift

To help you get started, we'd like to offer you a **free copy** of one of our bestselling ebooks:

www.bkconnection.com/welcome

When you claim your **free ebook**, you'll also be subscribed to our blog.

Our freshest insights

Access the best new tools and ideas for leaders at all levels on our blog at ideas.bkconnection.com.

Sincerely,

Your friends at Berrett-Koehler

Certified

Corporation